BIBLE TEA

GENESIS

---※---

VOLUME I

Kaydene Grant

Copyright © 2025 by Kaydene Grant

All rights reserved. No part of this publication may be reproduced, stored in a retrieval system, or transmitted in any form or by any means—electronic, mechanical, photocopying, recording, or otherwise—without the prior written permission of the publisher, except in the case of brief quotations embodied in critical articles or reviews.

Published by
Small House Publishing
Philadelphia, PA

www.sipbibletea.com

Scripture References

Unless otherwise noted, Scripture quotations are taken from the following translations:
Amplified Bible (AMP). Copyright © 1954, 1958, 1962, 1964, 1965, 1987 by
The Lockman Foundation.
www.Lockman.org

New King James Version (NKJV). Copyright © 1982 by Thomas Nelson.
All rights reserved.

King James Version (KJV). Public domain.

The retellings, commentary, and cultural reinterpretations within this book are the creative expressions of the author and are meant to invite readers into a fresh and familiar conversation with Scripture. This work is not intended to replace the Bible, but to help readers reimagine it with context, connection, and care.

ISBN: 979-8-9985933-4-5

Printed in the United States of America

Volume I

TABLE OF CONTENTS

PREFACE	VI
INTRODUCTION	XI
1. THE STORY OF ADAM & EVE GENESIS 1-3: THE BEGINNING	1
2. THE STORY OF CAIN & ABEL GENESIS 4:1-16: THE FIRST MURDER	11
3. THE STORY OF NOAH & THE ARK GENESIS 6: THE WICKED WORLD	13
4. THE FLOOD GENESIS 7-9	18
5. THE TOWER OF BABEL GENESIS 11: A BUNCH OF BABBLERS	22
6. THE STORY OF ABRAHAM GENESIS CHAPTER 12: GOD CALLS ABRAM	24
7. ABRAM & LOT GENESIS 13: THE GRASS AIN'T ALWAYS GREENER	29
8. ABRAM RECUES LOT GENESIS 14	32
9. ABRAM PROMISED A SON GENESIS 15	35

10. THE STORY OF ABRAM, SARAI & HAGAR — 39
    GENESIS 16: BABY MAMA DRAMA

11. ABRAM GETS A NEW NAME — 43
    GENESIS 17

12. THE STORY OF SODOM & GOMORRAH — 50
    GENESIS CHAPTER 19: LOTS SALTY WIFE

13. THE STORY OF ABRAHAM & ISSAC — 54
    GENESIS CHAPTER 21: ISSAC IS BORN

14. ABRAHAM'S SACRIFICE — 56
    GENESIS CHAPTER 22

15. ISSAC GETS A BRIDE — 59
    GENESIS CHAPTER 24

16. THE STORY OF JACOB & ESAU — 63
    GENESIS CHAPTER 25: THE TWINS

17. ISSAC & THE KING — 65
    GENESIS CHAPTER 26

18. TREACHEROUS TRICKERY — 68
    GENESIS CHAPTER 27

19. THE STORY OF JACOB, RACHEL & LEAH — 74
    GENESIS CHAPTER 28: JACOB'S SISTER WIVES

20. LYING LABAN — 83
    GENESIS CHAPTER 30

21. THE STORY OF JACOB & ESAU'S REUNION — 88
    GENESIS CHAPTER 30: JACOB'S FEAR

22. JACOB WRESTLES — 91
    GENESIS CHAPTER 32

23.	THE REUNION GENESIS CHAPTER 33	94
24.	THE TREACHERY CONTINUES GENESIS CHAPTER 34	97
25.	THE STORY OF JOSEPH GENESIS CHAPTER 37	101
26.	TAMAR & JUDAH GENESIS CHAPTER 38: DAUGHTER IN-LAWS REVENGE	106
27.	THE PRISON GENESIS CHAPTER 39	110
28.	THE PALACE GENESIS CHAPTER 41	115
29.	THE PURPOSE GENESIS CHAPTER 42	120
AFTERWORD		128
THE CAST LIST		130

Because the tea was hot from the beginning.

PREFACE

People always say that pastor's kids are the worst. I personally think that is an unfair stereotype. A stereotype that I spent my teenage years doing everything in my power to prove right! Wheeww, chiile. I was a mess! I got stories for days! Stories that I will never put down in writing so if you thought I was about to spill all the tea on myself I am so sorry to disappoint you. The one thing I will share is I was a rebel, and I never did anything the traditional way.

It all took place back in the 1900s. It was over thirty years ago so I have no idea exactly what year it was. My father, Bishop James Chalwell, started his church in the basement of one of his rental properties in Waterbury, Connecticut. A very small church with a heavy anointing. The members consisted of a melting pot of Caribbean islands: St. Kitts and Nevis, Antigua and Bermuda, Jamaica, Guyana, and my family from St. Thomas, USVI and Tortola, BVI.

We sang loud, sometimes a lil off key, but our harmonies bounced off the walls and penetrated deep into our souls. Handkerchiefs flew high in the air, foot stomps matched the calypso beat, and when the music stopped, the tambourines kept going. In this small basement church, my gift for telling Bible stories was born. One Sunday morning, my Sunday school teacher was trying to teach a lesson, but she was just loud and wrong! So, I kindly told her so. I think she was being sarcastic when she said, "Well you teach it then." But I was dead serious when I said, "OK" and proceeded to stand up and take her place.

I have no clue what the story was or exactly what I said, but I do know what happened afterwards. Everyone was laughing, she sat down, and my daddy said I could teach Sunday school from now on. By the time I was 18, I was a youth director, praise dance leader, on the praise and worship team, one of the drummers, and the children's church teacher. I was burned out!

Throughout the years visiting prophets would give me the same prophecy, I was going to be a mighty woman of God with a church without walls. I had no idea what that prophecy meant and by the time I was ready for college, I had no interest whatsoever to find out.

I left home and I buried all of my gifts.

Ten years later, I found myself searching for something that was missing. I was happily married, a boy mom, surrounded by friends that loved me, yet I felt completely lost. I started to reflect on the last time I really felt like myself, not a wife, not a mother, an employee, a friend, but just Kaydene. In my mind, I was taken back to being a teenager sitting with a bunch of church kids, teaching them Bible stories.

So, at the age of 28, I went on a spiritual journey. A journey to discover this mighty woman of God I was destined to be with a church without walls. By the age of 33, I got baptized again and fully dedicated my life to putting God first.

Four years later, I found myself angry at God. I was doing everything He instructed me to do. I was waking up at the crack of dawn and going LIVE on Instagram for morning devotions just for fifteen people to watch it. Shoutout to my day ones! I was making all kinds of content just for the same ten people to share it on Facebook. Thank you to my big sister Angelique for always sharing my content.

I stopped smoking weed, my Bible App streak was top tier, my fruits of the Spirit were giving pure fruitfulness, I even pushed past my church hurt and went back into ministry leadership with the dopest millennium ministry outchea, The Ethos Fam. Ayyerrr!

So, when is my turn, Lord? Who is this mighty woman of God? Where she at? Why do all these famous church leaders get to do their ministry full-time and I have to go back to being a teacher to help my husband pay the bills. I completely changed my dreams, my business, and my life to put God at the center.

So, when is it my turn, Lord? I literally asked this question in July of '22 at one of our ministry summer retreats. I heard God say one word to me, "Now!"

One month later, I went back home to visit my parents. As I was rummaging through their house looking for things I could steal...I mean borrow without returning. You know paper towel rolls, candles, food in the fridge that's not expired, some mugs because they literally have a million of them, I went into my father's office, and something caught my eye on his bookshelf.

I reached up and pulled down my old children's church book. *Bible Stories* by Martin Manser. As I opened the cover my mother's handwriting jumped from the page. She used that book to teach us, then used it to teach children church, then passed the book down to me when she passed me the torch to be the teacher.

I flipped through the book and landed on King David. As I read the story, I immediately burst out laughing. Kind David was a hot mess, chile. You mean to tell me he got somebody else's wife pregnant, tried to have the husband sleep with the wife to hide the fact she was already pregnant, and then when that didn't work, he made the general of the army put the husband on the front lines so he can get kilt! Tyler Perry ain't got nothing on this type of storytelling, hunty.

I immediately felt that nudge. The nudge I used to call my gut feeling but now I realize it's discernment. It's a sensitivity to actually hear what the Holy Spirit is telling you. I had this idea for a while to tell Bible stories again, but I didn't know how. I even had this dramatic sound saved on my phone. It was only 9 seconds long. Later I learned it was the intro to "WAP." Umm...that stands for worship and praise, mommy.

So, I picked up my phone and recorded three different clips of me reading the story and making crazy, confused, and flabbergasted faces. I figured out a way to write three sentences that would sum up the entire story but more importantly, I retold the story just like that little girl standing in front of her church proving that she understood what God was trying to tell us.

That video got twenty thousand views. So, I made another one. That got forty thousand views. In my third video I was in Honeygrow reading the story of Joseph and Potiphar's pedophile wife. That was my first video that got one million views. **Bible Tea** was officially born.

I knew I found my calling not because I kept going viral or my followers kept growing but because of my DMs. I have gotten hundreds of DMs from different people, different races, different ages, but all with the same message. **Bible Tea** has gotten them back into their word, and back into a close relationship with God. I finally understood what my prophecy of a church without walls really meant.

I would like to thank you for joining me on this **Bible Tea** journey. Thank you for constantly asking me when I was going to write this book. Thank you for all the hilarious comments and all the encouragement to keep going. Thank you for sharing my content and tagging your friends. Thank you for joining the Kweendom and tapping into morning devotion whether you're an, all the way *live* Kween at 5:30 a.m. EST or, a loyal replay Kween pon di replay.

Thank you for allowing this rebel pastor's kid to do things my way instead of the traditional way. To go against the status quo and spread God's word that makes church folks clutch their pearls. After all you know they say we are the worst.

INTRODUCTION

My Dearest Bible Tea Sippers,

If you bought this book thinking you were about to read flowery happily ever after Bible stories to your little children before they go to bed. This ain't that. If you bought this book thinking it was something other than actual Bible stories, like I wrote some original drama filled novel, this ain't that. If you bought this book thinking **Bible Tea** is only about the messiness of these Bible characters and that they aren't a direct reflection of your messy, disobedient, disrespectful self. This ain't that and that ain't this.

Bible Tea is a retelling of Bible stories using African American Vernacular English. It is the raw truth without chaser of what happened according to the word of God. It is in no shape or form a replacement for the Bible. You betta not think you can just read **Bible Tea** and not have to actually crack open your Bible and read the story for yourself.

This is *not* your typical Bible stories book. Where other books may skip over parts of these stories that may be deemed inappropriate, I not only included them I spilled all the tea, hunty. I spent *hours, days, weeks, and months* deep diving into Bible commentaries, biblical archives, researching Hebrew and Greek word meanings, and exploring historical context just to make sure I understood each story on a deeper level so that I can provide a lil extra tea for each of you.

2 Timothy 2:15 says, "Study and do your best to present yourself to God approved, a workman [tested by trial] who has no reason to be ashamed, accurately handling and skillfully teaching the word of truth."

You betta believe I did that! My prayer is as you sip on this **Bible Tea** that you just don't *read* the stories, but you *reflect* deeply on your own thoughts, emotions and actions. After all that's what T.E.A. stands for. I pray that you will read **Bible Tea** then read the actual story from the Holy Bible with a new perspective, passion, and purpose. The purpose of **Bible Tea** is to get you back into a close relationship with God. I want you to study and show yourself approved to God!

What perfect way to start than in the very first book of the Bible, Genesis. From the very beginning of time God desired a close intimate relationship with us. However, our doubt, delusions, disobedience, and dysfunctional patterns constantly draw us away from Him. From Adam and Eve all the way to Joseph, we see this happening over and over again throughout the book of Genesis. If we are completely honest, we can see the same patterns drawing us away from God in our lives. There are so many lessons we can learn from the first book of the Bible. So let us grab our teacups, put on the kettle, and pour out all the hot **Bible Tea** from Genesis. Welcome to **Bible Tea: Genesis.** Ain't no tea like **Bible Tea,** hunty.

~ Kaydene Grant | Coach Kbeau2ful

Chapter One
THE STORY OF ADAM & EVE
Genesis 1-3: The Beginning

SO, BOOM WHAT HAD HAPPENED WAS...

In the very, *very* beginning God created the heavens and the earth. The earth had no form whatsoever. There was nothing but darkness. The darkness was endless, and the Spirit of God hovered over the dark watery abyss. God said, "We need some light." So, boom there was light. And it was good. So, God separated the light from the darkness. He called the light day and the darkness night. So, from day one, there was evening time and morning time.

On the second day, God created the sky. The sky is like a barrier that separates the water beneath it and the moisture in the air. In other words, the earth now had an atmosphere. On the third day, God created dry land, plants, and beautiful green trees. And He was loving it! God said, "Yup, this is good." On the fourth day, God sprinkled stars in the sky. He created two large sources of light: one for the day, called the sun, and one for the night, called the moon. God was like, "This is some good stuff right here." On the fifth day, God created all the living creatures in the sea and all the flying creatures of the air. God said, "Y'all be good now. Make sure y'all multiply and fill all of the waters and the sky." On the sixth day of creation, God created all the living creatures on the land. He said that it was good.

Then God said, "Let Us create man in our own image." Yup, Jesus & the Holy Spirit were there too. So, He did, and it was good. But we'll get into that part later. But on the seventh day, God didn't create not a ting! He went to lay down somewhere because He needed to get some much-deserved rest. Now, let's rewind and go back to day six.

God created the earth, but He didn't let it rain yet because He wanted to create someone to take care of the ground. God wanted to create a human in His image. Everything else He created by speaking it into existence, but He did something special for man. God took the dust of the earth and molded it. He then breathed His very own breath into his nostrils and made him a living being. The Hebrew word *Adamah* means earth and soil. So, this newly created man now had a name. His name was Adam. God loved Adam *so* much.

God created a botanical garden and placed Adam in the garden so he could take care of it. I'm not talking 'bout some lil flower garden. I'm talking 'bout this garden was gorgeous, hunty!

There were four rivers flowing through it. Flowers and plants galore. Trees with juicy, scrumptious fruits were everywhere. Right smack dab in the middle of the garden was the Tree of Life and the Tree of Knowledge of Good and Evil. This was the Garden of Eden. Now, God gave this man *one job!* Just one dats it!

God told him, "Adam, listen. You can eat from *any* tree in this garden *except* from the Tree of Knowledge of Good and Evil. The day you eat from that tree, you finna die." That's the job y'all. God realized that Adam shouldn't be alone. God said, "You know what? It's not good for man to be alone. I'm 'bout to give him a helper. Let's see what will be suitable for him." The Lord gave Adam the task of naming every animal. But as He evaluated each animal, none of those animals was good enough to be Adam's helper. God needed to create another human to be the perfect match for Adam.

So, God put Adam to sleep. While Adam was knocked out and drooling, God took one of his ribs and created a new human. When Adam woke up and saw her, he was like, "Daaanngg, shawty! You are bone of my bone and flesh of my flesh. You are part of me, so I'm gonna call you *Woman*." Baaabbyy, life was *good*, good! Adam and his *Woman* were living their best lives! They were just buckey-nakey... everything just a swang-a-ling & dang-a-ling all over the place as they frolicked in the Garden of Eden.

God gave them dominion over *everything*. There was just one rule. They could eat everything *except* for one thing...Just *one* thing. Don't eat from the Tree of Knowledge of Good and Evil because then y'all finna die! They had *one* job. Just *one!* But then here came Satan with his sneaky, snake-self.

One day, Satan took the form of a serpent and slithered himself up to the *Woman*. Satan asked her, "Did God *really* say you can't eat from every tree up in here?" The *Woman* said, "We can eat all of 'em except for the one in the middle 'cause then we finna die." Satan was like, "Nah, you ain't gonna die, girl. God just knows when you do eat it, your eyes will open & you gonna be like gods." So, the *Woman* was like, "Well, it does look good, and I wanna be wise like a god. So, I'mma try it." No ma'am!

So, the *Woman* failed at her *one* job and ate from the forbidden tree. Then she gave some to Adam and his goofy self, ate it too. And just like that their eyes were opened, and man separated from God. Adam and his *Woman* looked down and realized they were naked. So, they threw some leaves together to make some outfits to cover up their shame. Little did they know, it wasn't their nakedness that was causing them shame.

Suddenly, they heard God taking His daily stroll in the Garden, so they quickly tried to hide. God called out to Adam, "Where are you?" Adam replied, "Oh heeyyy! We heard you coming, and we got scared because we were naked, so we hid." Bruh! So, God was like, "But who told you, you were naked tho? Did you eat from the tree I told you *not* to eat from?" Adam immediately shifted the blame. He said, "The *Woman you* gave me, gave me the fruit, so I ate it." God turned to the *Woman* and said, "What have you done?" The *Woman* replied, "The serpent deceived me!"

So, God laid down this curse:

The Fall

Serpent!
Smooth-tongued liar, slithering deceit.
You whispered death in Eden's heat.
Now the dust will be your feast,
Cursed beyond every beast.
Crawl! On your belly, no legs to stand.
A symbol of sin, a mark on the land.
From now 'til the end, war will rage,
Between your kind and the woman's wage.
Her Seed will crush your skull beneath,
And though you bite, it's just His heel you'll reach.
Woman!
Labor pain will follow where life begins.
Agony will twist through your bones, like your sins.
The ache will multiply, scream through your frame.
Yet still, you'll long for love in Adam's name.
But he will rule, and you will yearn,
A fire that flickers, but never burns.
Adam.
Dust-born. Breath-given. Soul-wrapped in flesh.
In my beautiful garden I gave you peace and rest.
You listened when you should have stood,
Ate what you knew you never should.
So now the ground drinks from your hand.
Cursed like you, cracked like man.
Thorns will rise where bread should bloom,

And sweat will carve out hunger's tomb.
To dust you came, to dust you'll go.
Every step a reminder, you shoulda said no.
No more Eden, no more rest.
Only toil, only death.

Adam and his *Woman* now were cursed with a new, hard life. Adam will have a life of hard labor. His *Woman* will now have pain when she gives birth, and always long for her husband, but he will rule over her. So, Adam finally named his *Woman* Eve, which means "source of life." They. Had. One. Job. God knew the heart of man. Now that man had an understanding of good and evil and could be tempted to choose evil, He did not want man to have access to the now forbidden Tree of Life. So, God clothed Adam and Eve and kicked them out of the Garden of Eden.

However, God had a redemption plan to bring His beloved humans back to a close relationship with Him. His redemption plan would come from a particular lineage of Adam's descendants. Our Redeemer would be Jesus Christ. But that's another tea for another day.

SIP ON THIS TEA: Here's some biblical context to sip on.

God's Redemption Plan

God was not playing when he dropped dem bars on Adam, Eve, and Satan. Everybody got cursed for their disobedience even the poor snake that Satan used to deceive Eve!

Let's sip on a particular scripture in this curse:

"And I will put enmity (open hostility) between you and the woman, and between your seed (offspring) and her Seed; He shall [fatally] bruise your head, and you shall [only] bruise His heel." (Gen. 3:15 AMP)

This is the very first prophecy of Jesus. God is saying that Satan and mankind will be enemies and have beef with each other for all generations. But God is saying that one day a savior will be born, redeem all mankind, and be victorious over Satan. The Devil and his little minions will try to destroy the Savior, like getting Him crucified on the cross , but it ain't gonna work because on the third day huunnttyyyy! He conquered death and rose victorious! In other words, Satan will bruise His heel, but Jesus will fatally crush Satan's head,

In Our Image

When God said, "Let us create man in our image," biblical scholars agree that God is referring to the Trinity. In case you don't know, the doctrine of the Trinity is that God is One in three Persons, God the Father, God the Son (Jesus Christ our Savior), and God the Holy Spirit.

So how are we created in God's image? Since the very beginning, God craved a close relationship with us, so He made us like Himself. Being made in God's image has nothing to do with our physical appearance. The image of God refers to the spiritual things that set us apart from the animal world. We have not only the ability to share our thoughts and feelings with our Creator, but we also have the ability to have close fellowship with Him. Being made in God's image gives the ability to make mental, moral, and social, intellectual choices so we can be in relationship with each other as well.

Satan's Trick

The Devil is a *liar!* He deceived Eve by using a little trick. His trick is simple but effective. He made her question what God said. That's it. That's the trick, and isn't it crazy that the Devil still uses that same ole trick with us! He starts whispering in our ears, making us question exactly what God said. Then he spins the word of God with a little lie mixed with a little truth to make it sound good. Then we find ourselves out here in these streets wearing camouflage outfits trying to fit in with the rest of the world when we were made to stand out. Wheeww, chiile!

Their Eyes Were Open

God is perfect, and everything He made was perfect. Adam and Eve's perspective was that everything was perfect too. Biblical scholars explain that when the scripture says, "their eyes were opened," it means their sin changed their perspective and separated them from perfection. They immediately realized their disobedience, and their disobedience changed how they viewed their world. What was once viewed as perfect now came with feelings of shame and fear.

Adam, Where You At?

First of all, God stays asking us questions that He already knows the answers to! His questions are not to obtain information because He already has all the info. His questions are to get us to realize something within ourselves. By asking Adam, "Where are you?" it wasn't just about His physical location. God already knew that man was hiding behind a bush with some leaf clothes on! God was asking Adam, "Where are you spiritually?" because I know we are now separated!

My Dearest Bible Tea Sippers, is God asking you the same question?

Chapter Two
THE STORY OF CAIN & ABEL
GENESIS 4:1-16: THE FIRST MURDER

SO, BOOM WHAT HAD HAPPENED WAS...

Adam and Eve had two sons named Cain and Abel. Abel was like a farmer; he dealt with the sheep, but Cain was like a gardener; he dealt with fruits. One day, Cain gave an offering to the Lord. He brought some of his fruits. Abel also brought an offering. He brought the finest firstborn out of all his flock and offered it to the Lord. God respected Abel for bringing his best, but He wasn't really feeling Cain's offering at all! Cain was all salty and mad! God was like, "Bruh, why are you mad and looking all pouty? Just do better! Do what's pleasing and acceptable to Me, and I'll accept it. *But* if you ignore what I'm asking, sin will start to creep in!"

So, you would think because God gave Cain another chance to come correct that he took that opportunity, right? Nope! Instead, Cain told Abel, "Yo, bro, let me holla at you real quick." (Sips tea loudly.) When they were alone in the field, Cain's backstabbing self attacked Abel and killed him. So, God was like, "Um, Cain, where's Abel"? God stay asking us questions that He already knows the answers to. Cain's disrespectful self was like, "I don't know! What, I look like his babysitter?"

Oop!

"What have you done? Your brother's blood cries out to Me from the ground! Now you will be cursed from the ground! Now the ground won't produce any crops for you. (It's giving starvation.) You're gonna be a vagabond. (It's giving broke & homeless.) From now on, you're gonna be a fugitive (It's giving exiled with no friends.) However, God was still merciful. God put a protective mark on Cain so when people saw him, they wouldn't try to kill him. And that's how the first murder happened. Eventually, Adam and Eve had more children. Their son, Seth, would one day have a descendant by the name of Abraham. But that's tea for another day.

My Dearest Bible Tea Sippers, you may be thinking, Why did God accept Abel's offering but not Cain's? Trust me, it has nothing to do with fruit compared to an animal sacrifice. This is a matter of the heart. Abel brought his very best to God. Even if Cain brought one hundred pieces of fruit compared to Abel's one lil animal, Abel's offering still would have been greater because of his obedient heart posture.

SIP ON THIS TEA: Here's some biblical context to sip on.

God honors obedience over sacrifice. Abel was obedient with God's request to always offer your absolute best to Him. God gave Cain the opportunity to correct his offering by being obedient and giving his best. But Cain allowed his anger to consume him, and just like God warned, sin crept in.

Chapter Three
THE STORY OF NOAH & THE ARK
GENESIS 6: THE WICKED WORLD

SO, BOOM WHAT HAD HAPPENED WAS...

Whenever we are reading the Bible and we see a list of names and numbers, we tend to just skip over them, don't we? Well, when we do that and just flip to the next page and move on to the next juicy story, we think we are still in the same timeline. That, my dear, is not the case. From the tragic tale of Cain and Abel to the adventure we're about to sip on, we have fast-forwarded 1,656 years.

To put it in perspective, the year I am writing this is The Year of Our Lord 2025. That means the events on the previous page would have happened in 369 AD. The world has changed a lot since then. The same holds true 1,656 years after God created Adam and Eve.

As humans continued to multiply on Earth, the sons of God looked at all the beautiful women running around and just could not resist! They were called the "sons of God", but they were anything but Godly, hunty. They took whoever they desired.

Their offspring the Nephilim (fallen ones/giants) ran amok. As a result, lust and violence spread through the earth like wildfire. God looked over the earth, and every person's heart was full of evil. He was completely heartbroken.

God's Reflection

In the beginning, I breathed life into clay.
Crafted humanity, showed them the way.
Yet now, their hearts have turned from Me,
Embracing corruption, blind to decree.
My Spirit won't contend with mortal's endless strife.
Their days are numbered, a fleeting life.
Witnessing wickedness spread vast and wide.
Every thought tainted; righteousness denied.
Regret fills My essence, sorrow deep and profound.
For the creation I cherished now desecrates the ground.
I'll cleanse the earth of all I've made.
From man to beast, all shall fade.
Yet, amidst the darkness, a glimmer of light.
Noah stands righteous in My sight.
Through him, a remnant shall endure.
A testament to grace, steadfast and pure.

Wheeww, chiile! God had enough! He declared that He would no longer allow His spirit to dwell in humans forever. His heart grieved the fact that He even created these disrespectful humans. Except for one. His name was Noah, and he was 500 years old. Our boy Noah was a righteous man. He didn't play about God. Regardless of what everyone else was doing, he stood ten toes down in righteousness. Noah had a wife and three sons named Shem, Ham, and Japheth.

One day God said to Noah:

Noah's Instructions

Noah, listen.
I've watched the earth unravel, seams torn at the edge.
Violence pouring from man's hands, staining every pledge.
The land cries out, bruised and worn.
Drowned in the wickedness it was never meant to adorn.
I will wipe it clean.
Not just the hands,
but the roots, the leaves, the sky.
Everything that breathes, that walks, that flies.
The storm is coming, rain unchained.
A flood so deep it'll erase My pain.
But you... you will build.
An ark from gopher wood, lined tight with pitch.
A vessel of promise, a covenant stitched.
Three hundred cubits long—My word in design,
Fifty in width, thirty in climb.
One window, one door, three levels tall,
A floating world before the fall.
A place for beasts, two by two, male and female,
My plan shines through.
Gather food, store it well.
For every wing, every paw, every shell.
This storm will rage, but you will stand.
The last of men, on the last dry land.

God was about to destroy the earth with a massive flood! Noah was not about to play any games. He got right to work. He followed God's instructions to the T. He gathered all the materials and built an ark longer than a football field and taller than a four-story apartment building. He gathered every animal and led them two by two. God made a covenant with Noah to save his family, so he grabbed his wife, his three sons, and their three wives and loaded them on too. When Noah finally finished the ark, he was 600 years old.

SIP ON THIS TEA: Here's some biblical context to sip on.

The Countdown 120 Years

Biblical scholars have a heated debate about this one. In verse 3 the amplified version reads:

> "Then the LORD said, 'My Spirit shall not strive *and* remain with man forever, because he is indeed flesh [sinful, corrupt given over to sensual appetites]; nevertheless, his days shall yet be a hundred and twenty years.'"(Gen. 6:3 AMP)

What exactly does one hundred twenty years mean? Scholars have two theories:

Theory One: The mentioned one hundred twenty years is declaring that humans will no longer live long lives like Noah's tales-from-the-crypt old self. This theory holds some weight because, after Noah's family, people no longer live past 200 years old. We sure nuff don't live that long in modern times.

Theory Two: The mentioned one hundred twenty years is declaring that God is counting down how many years is left until he destroys the earth with the flood. Many scholars say it took Noah one hundred twenty years to build the ark based on this theory. I'm not a math whiz, but when Noah started building he was 500 years old. When the flood finally came, he was 600 years old. It's giving one hundred years to build the ark, not one hundred twenty, but that's just me. I encourage you to do your own studying and choose whichever theory matches your research.

Sons of God

I can't even begin to explain how exciting this particular tea makes me. From the 7th grade all the way to my high school graduation, I was a Classical Magnet Scholar. We studied Greek and Roman culture and mythology for years! Shoutout to my Classical friends! Bible scholars have many theories on exactly who the sons of God are mentioned here. My absolute favorite theory is that they are fallen angels. Fallen angels who were on earth running amok and having babies with humans. These babies became giants. Supernatural beings with great strength. Sure, sounds like Hercules, huh? It's just a fun theory that I love to go down the rabbit hole with. I encourage you to do your own research and choose which theory matches your biblical search for truth.

My Dearest Bible Tea Sippers, I must share an epiphany that changed my perspective on something particularly important: the mythological gods and goddesses are rooted in astrology. So, if they were indeed the fallen angels that fell with Satan, why on earth would I identify myself according to my astrology sign? Umm...hmm. Y'all not ready for that cup of tea. I guess we can sip on that another day.

Chapter Four
THE FLOOD
GENESIS 7-9

SO, BOOM WHAT HAD HAPPENED WAS...

When the ark was finished, God said to Noah, "It's about to go down! In just seven days, I'm about to make it rain! I need you to take these animals and your family and get ready to go!" The animals came to Noah just like God said they would. Noah and his family boarded the ark, and then God, *shut the door!* Then God started singing, "Sunny days, everybody loves them, tell me, baby, can you stand the rain? Storms will come, this we know for sure; can you stand the rain!" That's a new edition song for all my holies that don't know secular music.

Ok, God didn't sing that, but it did rain! And when I say rain, I'm talking about it rained for forty days and forty nights. The water got so high it was twenty feet above the highest mountain.

Errthang and *errbody* died. The waters covered the earth for one hundred fifty days. That's about five months. When God finally closed the windows of heaven and turned off the faucet of the deep underground springs, the waters receded, and the ark came to rest on top of a mountain.

After another five months, you could finally see the mountaintops. So, Noah opened up a window and sent out birds. You see, if the birds could find a place to land, then Noah knew the water was all gone. But dem birds kept coming back to him. He waited another seven days, then sent out birds again, but they came back. He waited another seven days. This time, when he sent out the dove, it didn't return! Finally, Noah opened the door to the ark and saw that the ground was dry.

When Noah finally came out of the ark, he was 601 years old. He built an altar and made a sacrifice to the Lord. God's heart mourned the destruction of the flood. God vowed to never curse His beautiful Earth again based on the wickedness of humans. God told Noah and his sons to multiply and fill the earth. As a reminder of His promise, he created a symbol in the sky—a beautiful, colorful rainbow.

Now, Noah done been through a lot! He had to build an ark for one hundred years. He was stuck in an ark with a bunch of filthy animals. Not only was he stuck with a whole zoo, but he was in that ark for a year with his wife, his three sons, and their wives. I don't know about y'all, but I ain't trying to be stuck nowhere with my family *and* my in-laws at the same time! So, what did he decide to do to cope with all this PTSD? Noah got in his farmer's bag and planted a vineyard.

Chiile, Noah made him some wine and got turnt up! He was so drunk he passed out buckey nakey in his tent. Now, his son Ham came into the tent and saw him. When he told his brothers that Pops was passed out drunk, with all his junk hanging out like a tree trunk, they entered into the tent backwards and respectfully covered Noah up.

Now, the next morning, hungover Noah was livid at what happened. He cursed Ham's son Canaan to a life of slavery! He blessed his other two sons and made Canaan their slave! Yikes!

Noah lived 350 more years, then finally died when he was 950 years old.

SIP ON THIS TEA : Here's some biblical context to sip on.

The Promise

Although we call it a rainbow, in fact the Hebrew translation of the word used in this scripture is "War Bow." God rained down harsh judgment on the entire earth. Literally! It is as if He went to war on all the evil on the earth and clearly won hands down!

But God is full of grace and mercy. He promised to never destroy the earth again by flood. As a reminder, he gave us a beautiful colorful symbol of his War Bow in the sky. I once read a beautiful poem that said there is no arrow in the war bow because when God shot it in the sky, the arrow turned away from us and went straight into his own heart. That makes me love rainbows even more!

Ham's Deed

My Dearest Bible Tea Sippers, there are just some biblical mysteries we may never know. But that sure doesn't stop biblical scholars from arguing about it.

There are three major theories on exactly what went down in Noah's tent when he was drunk and unconscious. (Sips tea quietly.)

Theory One: Ham literally saw his father naked, and instead of honoring his father and respectfully covering him up, he ran out and told his brothers in a ridiculing manner. His brothers were not going for his disrespect, so they entered backwards so they wouldn't see all of their father's goods hanging out and covered him with dignity.

But these other theories, chiile! (Sips tea loudly.)

Theory Two: Ham goes into the tent and, "sees his father's nakedness." Some Bible commentaries try to explain that this phrase means Ham sexually assaulted his father.

Theory Three: Ham goes into the tent and "uncovered Noah's nakedness" by sleeping with Noah's wife.

My Dearest Bible Tea Sippers, in all honesty all the contextual evidence I reviewed does not point to this second or third theory. These commentaries try to use a scripture in Leviticus Chapter 18 that says, "Thou shall not uncover nakedness..." This scripture lays out all the prohibited ways you should not have incest. It even includes not having sex with your father's wife, whether she was your mama or not. They was *wild* wild!

The reason I don't think these theories fit is because the Hebrew word for see and uncover are two completely different words. So, I tend to lean more towards the first theory. Of course, you just can't take my word for it. You must get into to the word and sip on this one for ya self!

Chapter Five
THE TOWER OF BABEL
GENESIS 11: A BUNCH OF BABBLERS

SO, BOOM WHAT HAD HAPPENED WAS...

Fast forward one hundred years after the flood. Everybody on the earth spoke the same language. Although they were given instruction to multiply and fill the earth, they were always chilling amongst each other. One day, one of Noah's grandsons, Nimrod, gathered some people together. (Gen.10:10) The people decided to get all fancy, take some clay, and throw it in the fire to make it hard and strong. They done discovered how to make bricks, y'all. They started talking to each other, brainstorming how they could use these bricks to build instead of stone. God was just looking down at these humans like, "Here we go with the shenans. If they shenan once, they gonna shenanigan."

Next the people dem decided to take some tar and put it between the bricks so that they can build a city. These people were advancing technologically. *Umm...hmm.* Sounds familiar. Once they built the city, they then got the bright idea to build a tower. Not some lil' skyscraper, hunty. Oh no. These fools decided they wanted to build a tower so tall it would reach up to the sky. They wanted to make a name for themselves and build a city where everyone could live together, and no one would ever have to leave. But that was not their instruction! They were supposed to spread over the entire Earth and multiply—not sit around playing real-life monopoly, building cities and stuff.

God said, "Absolutely not! This is only the beginning of some hot mess. You know what? They are too unified because they speak the same language. Let us scramble up their languages so they can't understand each other."

So, the Lord scattered their tongues, then scattered them away from their lil' brick city. That's why I think that city and the tower were called Babel, 'cause they left there doing nothing but a bunch of babbling.

SIP ON THIS TEA: Here are some personal reflections to sip on.

What's Your T.E.A.? Thoughts. Emotions. Actions

Not every opportunity is a God opportunity. Just like the folks at Babel, we get caught up building things that look good but have nothing to do with God's will. Their plan made sense on paper—unity, progress, elevation—but their hearts were off. It was about pride, not purpose.

My Dearest Bible Tea Sippers, how many towers have we started building just to prove a point or make a name for ourselves? God will shut it *all* down if it means saving you from yourself.

Take a minute. What are you building? Is God in it?

Journal your T.E.A.—sort out your *Thoughts*, name those *Emotions*, and take some *Action* that leads to alignment, not ego.

Chapter Six
THE STORY OF ABRAHAM
GENESIS CHAPTER 12: GOD CALLS ABRAM

SO, BOOM WHAT HAD HAPPENED WAS...

One of Noah's descendants was a man named Terah. Terah had three sons: Abram, Nahor, and Haran. Haran had a son named Lot and a daughter named Milcah. Unfortunately, Haran died, so his brother Nahor took Milcah as his wife. Abram took a woman named Sarai as his wife, and Terah decided to move all of his family to a new land.

Now in the new land the Lord said to Abram:

The Calling
Go!
Leave your land, leave your kin,
Leave the place where your past begins.
Walk by faith, not by sight,
Step into promise, step into light.
I will show you—watch, believe,
A land unknown, but destined for thee.
No need for a map, no need for a plan,
Just trust in My voice, the work of My hand.

I will make you great, your name will rise,
Set apart, a light in their eyes.
Not for riches, not for pride,
But so through you, My love won't hide.
I will bless you—abundantly, bold,
Favor like rain, more than you hold.
But hear Me now, this is the test:
I bless you, so you bless the rest.
Who lifts you up? I lift them higher.
Who brings you low? They taste My fire.
My wrath on those who bring disgrace,
But to the humble—mercy, grace.
And through you, the nations will see,
A blessing that flows eternally.
All tribes, all tongues, from death to birth,
Will taste this blessing, across the whole earth.

God stays with the bars, um, kayyy! Abram was obedient and left right away. At the age of 75, he packed up all his belongings, all his servants, his wife Sarai, and his nephew Lot, and headed to the land of Canaan. However, when Abram arrived in Canaan, the land wasn't empty! It was full of the people called the Canaanites. But the Lord appeared to Abram and said, "I'm gonna give this land to your descendants!"

Now, Sarai was barren. She couldn't have any children. But that didn't stop Abram from believing in God. He believed what God said to him. To prove it, he built an altar right there where God appeared to him. Abram then moved on to other lands and wherever he pitched his tent he built an altar and had a good ole time worshiping God thru prayer, praise, and thanksgiving. Now that's how you thank God in advance ok! But a severe famine struck the land! So, Abram went to Egypt to live temporarily. When he was about to enter Egypt, he told his wife, "Look here! You look so good, girl! You are a baddie! When these Egyptians see you, they are gonna kill me just to have you for themselves. So, if anyone asks you, I need you to tell them you're my sister, so they don't kill me!"

Sure nuff, when the Egyptians saw Sarai, they were going crazy for her. Even the Pharaoh's princes—more like his pimps—reported to him about how beautiful she was. So, the Pharaoh *tooketh* Sarai and placed her in his house of harems. That's a house for all his wives and side chicks! The Pharaoh didn't just take her, he paid Abram *very well* for Sarai. I'm talking 'bout Abram was now wealthy with donkeys, sheep, oxen, camels, and even his own male and female servants! (Sips tea with a side eye.)

But God was not having this! God rained down plagues on the Pharaoh's household because he took Sarai. The Pharaoh called Abram like, "Bruh, what did you do to me? Why did you lie and say this jawn was your sister? Man, take your wife and get outta here! Y'all gotta go!" So, Pharaoh had his men escort Abram and Sarai and everything they had out of Egypt.

SIP ON THIS TEA: Here's some biblical context to sip on.

God's Promise

Go. It seems like such a simple word, but it's a complicated command. Let's break it down. God is asking Abram to leave his homeland, all of his family, and his father's household. Which means, if he chooses to go, he is also making the choice to abandon his inheritance, his lineage, his support system, and if we're honest, his comfortability. He's told to leave all this to go to a land that God will show him. But when he gets there, he realizes that the land isn't his yet. Which means his destination is actually a part of his future destiny, not a place he can presently dwell in. (Chiile, that will preach!) On top of that, God keeps talking about Abram's descendants when his wife is barren! Yet, despite what this present looks like, Abram believes God's promises about his future, and Abram makes the decision to go!

The Whole Earth Will Be Blessed

Here's the real tea about this covenant that God made with Abram. God is telling Abram that everyone on this entire earth will be blessed through his descendants. You may be thinking, My Dearest Bible Tea Sippers, how is it possible that those disrespectful Israelites that we constantly read about in the Bible could possibly bless the entire world? It's not *all* of his descendants just one extremely important person that would come from Abram's lineage, the Messiah, Jesus Christ. It's through Jesus that this promise is fulfilled. The blessing that the entire world will get to receive is the gift of salvation. That's the real tea! But I promise we will sip on that another day.

Abram Deceives the Pharaoh

Biblical scholars say Sarai was about 65 years old at this time. When you keep reading in Genesis chapter 20, we discover that Sarai is actually his half-sister. They have the same father but different mothers. However, a *half*-truth is a *whole* lie! It's a deceptive statement that leaves out important information. Sarai was indeed his wife, and as we learned, there were grave consequences for Abram's deception! Unfortunately, this isn't the last time we will see this level of cunningness from Abram.

Abram's Gifted Wealth

Now hear me out, Bible Tea Sippers. I went deep into the rabbit hole for this biblical context. I read Christian, Jewish, and Muslim scholars' thoughts on my theory. I'm going to encourage y'all to do your own Bible study if you disagree with me here, and maybe we can discuss it during a Bible Tea-Tea party. With that being said, here's my theory:

Abram got wealthy as payment from the Pharaoh for Sarai. Part of that payment was male and female Egyptian servants. They were then instructed to take everything and get outta Egypt. This tells me that Hagar, oh wait, we haven't got to her yet. Oops. That's another Bible Tea for another day.

Chapter Seven
ABRAM & LOT
GENESIS 13: THE GRASS AIN'T ALWAYS GREENER

SO, BOOM WHAT HAD HAPPENED WAS...

Abram left Egypt, beaucoup rich. (I had to google how to spell beaucoup whole time I thought it was boo-koo, chiile.) So, he returned to Bethel. The same place where he first set up a tent and altar to praise God. But his nephew Lot, aka Lotty, was also a lil rich now too. He had lots of flocks and herdsmen.

Now, what happens when you got a whole bunch of people and stuff occupying the same space? Yup! They start arguing and fighting with each other. To make matters worse, the Canaanites and other tribes had livestock too. The land could not support all these hungry animals.

Abram didn't want all that drama to ever come between him and his nephew. He told Lotty to pick wherever he wanted to go, and he would go in the opposite direction. Lotty looked around and saw that the Valley of Jordan was all plush and green. So, Lotty pitched his tents there, facing the city of Sodom. *Umm...hmm.*

God said to Abram:

The Promise
Lift your eyes, take a guest,
North and south, east, and west.
Everywhere your feet may step,
It is yours—forever blessed.
Walk on, walk on,
Step by step, faith stays strong.
Walk on, walk on,
What I give will not be gone.
Your seed will rise like dust in the air,
Too many to count, too great to compare.
If a man could number every grain of sand,
Then he could measure what's in My hand.
Walk on, walk on.
All that you see.
Walk on, walk on,
It's destined to be.

SIP ON THIS TEA: Here's some biblical context to sip on.

Lot's Choice

If the grass ain't always greener on the other side was a person, it would be Lot. Lot immediately made the choice to choose the land that looked plusher for himself. The Bible states in verse 13 that the men of Sodom were exceedingly evil in the sight of the Lord. Biblical scholars agree that surrounding cities would have been aware of what type of city Sodom was.

Lot not only chose what seemed to be the more fertile land, but he also pitched his tent willingly toward the city that he knew was not pleasing to God.

How many times have we been in proximity to things and people we know aren't pleasing to God with the foolish thought that we are strong enough to not let it affect us. Ha! Lot did the same thang! He chose the land that had more water and was closer to what he thought was a lavish city despite it being wicked. He would soon learn he made the wrong choice.

Chapter Eight
ABRAM RECUES LOT
GENESIS 14

My Dearest Bible Tea Sippers, once again I must take a brief moment to spill a lil extra tea. You may be under the impression that Abram was this very gentle, understanding, peaceful man that would rather go separate ways than get caught up in any fighting. Ha! That is until someone kidnapped his nephew!

SO, BOOM WHAT HAD HAPPENED WAS...

A bunch of kings were about to go to war! Let's call one side The Four Kings and the other side The Five Kings. Now, The Four Kings included the King of Elam, who was the most powerful. The Five Kings included the King of Sodom and the King of Gomorrah. Stay with me, it gets good.

For 12 years, all eight kings served the King of Elam, but in the thirteenth year, The Five Kings decided to join together in rebellion. They went wild, conquering all the surrounding cities. Finally, when it was time to fight against The Four Kings, they met at the valley of Siddim. You would think it's Five Kings against Four, that's an easy win, right? Well, it just so happened that the valley was full of tar pits! So, as The Five Kings attacked, the King of Sodom and the King of Gomorrah fell into the tar pits! Chiile, them other three kings just left them in the tar and ran away! They was stuck on stupid literally!

The Four Kings were like, "Welp! That was easy!" and captured everything in Sodom and Gomorrah. I'm talking about they took all the food, provisions, and the people! They took everybody, including a certain person who was living there called Lotty! *Umm...hmm.*

But a survivor got away and ran straight to Abram. When he heard what happened to his young boi, he gathered up three hundred and eight of his trained men. Abram himself led the charge as they chased them down and attacked them into the night. They not only won, but they also got back all the possessions, all the people, and his nephew Lot. Now, the Tar King, I mean, the King of Sodom was all hype and was trying to give Abram all kinds of gifts. But Abram was like, "Nah, I'm good. You're not about to say you're the one that made me rich. I made a covenant with God, so I ain't taking anything from you." And that's how Abram proved just because he's laid back, it doesn't mean he won't lean forward real quick!

SIP ON THIS TEA: Here are some personal reflections to sip on.

What's Your T.E.A.? Thoughts. Emotions. Actions

Wheew ,Chiile. Do you have the one friend or family member that it seems like you always gotta bail them out of suttin? Sometimes we're so quick to bail people out, we block the lesson God's trying to teach them. Love your people, yes—but every rescue ain't your assignment. Read the part again slowly.

My Dearest Bible Tea Sippers, the next time they call you I need you to stop and ask yourself some questions. Ask yourself: Am I helping or enabling? Is this compassion or control? Do they really want help or am I just their plan B for when they knowingly make wrong decisions?

Journal your T.E.A.—check your *Thoughts*, process your *Emotions*, and take *Action* that includes healthy boundaries. Everybody can't keep calling *you* when their choices blow up.

Chapter Nine
ABRAM PROMISED A SON
GENESIS 15

SO, BOOM WHAT HAD HAPPENED WAS...

One day God appeared to Abram in a vision and said, "Don't be scared! I'm always going to shield you! You're reward for your obedience is going to be crazy!" But Abram was kinda feeling his age creep up on him. Not to mention his sister, I mean his wife Sarai was still barren.

He said:

Abram's Plea
Lord God!
What's left for me?
What reward do I hold when my hands stay empty?
I walk in favor, I walk in grace,
But no son, no heir—just time and space.
Look at me!
I've built, I've worked, I've stayed in Your light.
But who carries my name when I say goodnight?
Eliezer? A servant? One born in my walls?
Is this the legacy after all?

(Somebody needs to lay some tracks to all these bars I be dropping.) So, God took Abram and made him look up at the sky and in his Mufasa voice he said, "All that the light touches…" Nah, it was more like:

The Covenant
Eliezer? Nah he won't carry your name.
That dude is a servant. That ain't the game.
What I promised? It still stands.
A son from your body, formed by My hands.
Look up at the stars, try to count them if you can.
Too many to number, each one countless, like grains of sand.
That's your legacy. That's your seed.
You're descendant so many too vast to see.

God also reminded him of his first promise, the inheritance of land. Abram believed what God said, but he still asked for proof. So, God instructed him to gather some animals, cut them for a sacrifice/ritual, and wait for an answer. Now, Abram was waiting so long that it became nighttime, and he fell into a deep sleep. God gave him his answer in a dark scary vision.

God's prophecy went like this:

The Promise in Darkness

Know for sure.
This ain't a guess, ain't a dream, ain't a test.
Your seed will suffer, they won't find rest.
Strangers.
Foreign feet on Egyptian land,
Bound in chains by another man's hand.
They will serve, they will bow,
Four hundred years— but I'll free them somehow.
I see the pain, I count the cries,
I hear the blood that stains the skies.
But when the time is full, when the weight is real,
I will judge, I will strike, I will make them kneel.
And your seed will rise, their backs made strong,
They'll leave that place wealthy,
walkin' where they belong.
As for you,
You'll rest in peace, your days stretched wide,
Sleep with your fathers, no fear, no pride.
But hear Me now, in the fourth generation,
I'll bring them back—to their foundation.
Canaan will be theirs, My word stands true,
But the Amorites still have their injustice to do.

And that, My Dearest Bible Tea Sippers, is foreshadowing what's to come in the Book of Exodus. But that's another Bible Tea *book* for another day.

SIP ON THIS TEA: Here are some personal reflections to sip on.

What's your T.E.A.? Thoughts. Emotions. Actions.

Abraham was like, "So, you still gon' bless me cuz it's giving nah." That was *real*. Waiting on God will have you questioning everything—even what He *promised*.

But just because it's taking long doesn't mean God changed His mind. He didn't forget. He's just building your faith in the silence.

My Dearest Bible Tea Sippers, please be honest—what have you started doubting just because it's delayed?

Journal your T.E.A.—be real about your *Thoughts,* sit with your *Emotions,* and take *Action* by choosing faith over frustration.

Chapter Ten
THE STORY OF ABRAM, SARAI & HAGAR
GENESIS 16: BABY MAMA DRAMA

SO, BOOM WHAT HAD HAPPENED WAS...

Abram and his wife Sarai are old geezers at this point. Sarai was becoming impatient waiting on God's promise. So, one day out the blue she says to Abram, "Look sir, just take my Egyptian maid Hagar, sleep with her, and since she's my slave, her child will be my child and that's how I'll finally get my baby!" Ma'am! You doing too muucchh! Abram was like, "Umm, ok whatever you say wife."

Abram took Hagar and made her his side piece. When Hagar found out she was pregnant she started looking at Sarai with contempt. Sarai felt like Hagar was walking around the house acting like the main chick and not the side piece. She didn't like how she kept looking at her all sideways.

Sarai went to Abram and was like, "Nah, this chick is in my house thinking she's somebody, and it's all your fault! I gave you my maid, and once she found out she was pregnant, she's acting like she's better than me, which is disrespectful. (Sips tea softly while staring over my glasses.) Abraham's punk self was like, "She's your slave, do whatever you want!" So, Sarai got all up in Hagar's face and dealt with her harshly! Hagar was like, "This is toxic. I'm out!"

As Hagar was running away, an Angel showed up and was like, "Yooo, Hagar, where you coming from and where you going?" She was like, "Anywhere but here, I gotta get away from my mistress Sarai." The angel was like, "Nah, boo! You need to go back and submit, 'cause God is gonna bless you too. You're going to have a son named Ishmael, and many descendants will come from you!"

The angel declared:

Ishmael's Prophecy
Behold!
You carry life, a son inside,.
A name already spoken, a name that won't hide.
Ishmael—God hears! Every cry, every tear, every pain, every fear.
The Lord has seen, the Lord has known,.
Your suffering ain't been left alone.
But hear this— Your son won't bow, won't break, won't bend.
He'll move like the wind, a storm with no end.
A wild donkey of a man, free but untamed,
A fighter, a force, no leash, no chain.
His hand against men, and theirs against him,
Conflict his shadow, war in his skin.
He won't seek peace, he won't blend in,
He will stand apart—defiant to kin.

Hagar was all emotional and was like, "God sees me even when other people don't." She returned home and gave birth to a son and named him Ishmael, which means, "God hears." Abram was 86 years old when Ishmael was born.

SIP ON THIS TEA: Here's some biblical context to sip on.

Hagar the Egyptian Maid

Finally, I get to spill the tea on my theory about Hagar. So, as I mentioned before, Sarai got kidnapped and placed into the Pharaoh's hoe house. Imagine being taken against your will and given to the Pharaoh so he can have his way with you. She must have been terrified! But that didn't happen. Why? Because God intervened with plagues and Pharaoh released her. *But* Abram still got rich as payment for the Pharaoh taking his wife. Part of that payment was (drumroll please) Egyptian servants, aka Hagar!

So, Sarai knows *exactly* what it feels like to be taken against your will and given to a man so he can have his way with you, and she still turned around and did the same thing to Hagar. Then had *thee* audacity to get mad when Hagar felt contempt towards her. Ma'am! Hagar didn't ask for any of this. This was your crazy behind impatient plan, not hers. I mean, Hagar started tripping when she was feeling herself, but it's your fault, not Hagar's! Wheeww, chiile! I had to get that off my chest. Now back to biblically sound contextual evidence and not just theories based on other religious texts and my anger.

Consequences of Sarai's Plan

If Abram was 86 years old when Ishmael was born, that means Sarai was 76 years old. She understandably was growing impatient. But there's a huge difference between feeling impatient and trying to make your own moves instead of waiting on God. Her impatient plan had grave consequences.

According to biblical scholars, a popular theory is that Arabic Muslims are direct descendants of Ishmael! That's right, the three Abrahamic religions—Judaism, Christianity, and Islam—all derive from Sarai's impatient plan. All from some baby mama drama!

Chapter Eleven
ABRAM GETS A NEW NAME
GENESIS 17

SO, BOOM WHAT HAD HAPPENED WAS...

Fast forward. Now Abram is 99 years old. That's a whole century!

God appears to him again with a new covenant:

Covenant of Circumcision
I am God Almighty.
Walk before Me— blameless, whole.
Humble soul know My presence, feel My call.
I am the One who holds it all.
I make a covenant, sealed and true,
Between Me and you, through all you do.
I will multiply, make nations rise.
Kings will walk beneath your skies.
No more Abram— Your name is changed.
Abraham!
A father's name.
Through you, descendants spread like sand.
This land you walk—it's in your hand.

Canaan's soil, its hills, its breath,
An everlasting place of rest.
But hear Me now—this vow is signed,
Marked in flesh, a holy line.
Circumcised—this is the sign,
A cut, a mark, a bond divine.
Every son, eight days old,
Shall bear this sign—My promise told.
Born in your house, bought with your gold,
Every man, forever bold.
And Sarai?
No longer Sarai, but Sarah stands.
A mother of kings, of mighty lands.
She will bear a son, and in that child,
My covenant lives, My plan is wild.
Isaac! Laughter—joy made real,
Through him, My promise is revealed.
Ishmael?
Blessed, but not the heir.
A nation strong, but Isaac's share.
One year's time—watch it be.
The promise stands—walk with Me.

Abraham was so happy he fell on his face, laughing and worshiping God. Not only did he and his wife have a new name, but they finally were going to have their son. In just one year, God promised that Sarah would give birth to a son named Isaac. However, Abraham also pleaded with God to bless his son Ishmael. God was clear that His chosen people would come from the lineage of Isaac, not Ishmael, but God honored his request and gave a blessing to Ishmael.

There was just one little thing, though—God created a new circumcision covenant to show who His chosen people will be. All males, eight days old and older, had to be snippity-snipped! So, in order to honor God's new covenant, Abraham made every male servant in his household get circumcised. Including his 13-year-old son Ishmael and his 99-year-old wrinkled self. Lawd, have mercy!

Sometime later, Abraham was chilling outside of his tent. Suddenly, he saw three men walking toward him. He ran up to them and bowed straight down. He said, "Please don't leave here without stopping by and chilling with me. I'm gonna have my servants grab some water to wash y'all feet, and y'all can relax out of the sun right under the tree." Abraham ran into the tent straight to Sarah and said, "Wife! I need you to whip up some cakes. I'm going to prepare some food for our guest." When he placed their meal in front of them, the men asked for Sarah. But she was still in the tent ear hustling. They said, "We're going to return to you in exactly one year, and your wife Sarah will have a son."

Now, nosey behind Sarah overheard this and busted out laughing. She said to herself, "Puh-lease! I am too old and so is my husband. You think we still be getting down like that? I am too old to get pregnant." Immediately, one of the men said, "Oh, Sarah thinks we got jokes or something? Why is she laughing and saying she's too old to get pregnant? Is there anything that is too hard for God?" Sarah was shooketh! She got so scared because she realized that these were not some ordinary men! And she was right! She immediately started backpedaling, talking 'bout, "No, I wasn't laughing." The Lord corrected her and said, "You definitely laughed." With that, the men got up to leave and started heading toward Sodom. As they walked, The Lord said to the two angelic beings with Him.

God Judges Sodom
Shall I keep this from Abraham?
My friend, My chosen, My righteous man?
Through him, nations rise, the world is blessed.
His name will stand, his house is set.
I have known him. Called him Mine, set him apart,
To teach his sons, to guard their hearts.
To walk in justice, to lead with truth,
To keep My ways, to bear My fruit.
But listen—
The cries of Sodom, they shake the ground.
The weight of sin is circling 'round.
Their wickedness screams in the night.
A city drenched in endless vice.
So, I will go.
I will see.
I will judge what comes to Me.
If their sin is what they claim,
Then fire falls—and none remain.

The two angels immediately left and headed for Sodom. Abraham was really worried! God had just told him His plan to destroy the entire city of Sodom! His young boi Lotty lives there! He said to the Lord, "Are you really about to destroy the entire city? What if you find fifty righteous people there?" God was like, "Alright, bet! I'll save it if I find fifty righteous people."

So, then Abraham was like, "Alright, Lord, what if you find about forty-five or let's say like twenty righteous people?" God said, "Okay. If I find forty-five or even twenty righteous people, I won't destroy it."

So then Abraham was like, "Don't be mad, okay? But just hear me out. What if you only find like ten righteous people? How about that?" At that point, God was like, "I will save it even if I only find *ten* righteous people." And then *poof!* God disappeared. Abraham returned to his home, probably feeling all hopeful. After all, it can't be that hard to find ten righteous people, right? (Sips tea loudly.)

SIP ON THIS TEA: Here's some biblical context to sip on.

The Covenant of Circumcision

The word circumcise means, "cut around." Circumcision is a surgery to cut off the foreskin from a man's dang-gaah-lang. (Chokes on tea laughing.)

Circumcision was a serious religious rite required of all Abraham's descendants to signify God's covenant with him. Circumcision identified God's chosen people from everyone else. Eventually the Mosaic Law also included this covenant.

The Three Guests

Biblical scholars widely agree that God often visited earth in a human form. This is called *theophany*. According to Dr. Britannica, (Yes, the Encyclopedia) Theophany comes from the Greek word *theophaneia* which means appearance of God.

Theophany is defined as the appearance of God to human beings. Many scholars believe this particular appearance was Jesus Himself making a cameo appearance all the way in Genesis. I absolutely love this theory because it proves Jesus preexisted before the New Testament. Genesis proves John 1:1 that says, "In the beginning was the word. And the word was with God and the word was God." Yes, Jesus was there before the world was even created and made pop up appearances before his earthly birth. Keep an eye out for more theophanies as we sip some more.

Sarah's Laughter

Now you may be thinking, "How come when Abraham laughed when God told him he was about to have a son in a year, God was cool, but when Sarah laughed, He corrected her?" Well, My Dearest Bible Tea Sippers, this is a matter of the heart. When Abraham laughed, he was full of joy, and he truly believed God's promise. Sarah, on the other hand, laughed out of pure disbelief. She's been waiting on this promise not for weeks or months or even years. It's been decades!

Let's break this down:

- Abraham left his father's at 75 years old that means Sarah was 65 years old.

- Pharaoh kidnapped her shortly after.

- Abraham had Ishmael at 86 years old which means Sarah is 76 years old.

- Ismael is 13 years old when he gets circumcised which means Abraham is 99 years old and Sarah is 89 years old.

- Men appear and tell them they will have a son in one year, which means Sarah will be 90 years old when she gives birth.

How many of y'all would burst out laughing too? We don't know how long Abraham and Sarah were married before God told them to leave Abraham's family. But if the math is mathing, we at least know she's been waiting twenty-five long years for this promise.

It's only human to laugh in disbelief. But God don't play about doubting Him. In her waiting, Sarah forgot *who* she was waiting on. In her waiting, she started looking at her present predicament instead of the promise. God said what He said. His word never comes back void. Sarah needed that reminder, and so do we!

Chapter Twelve
THE STORY OF SODOM & GOMORRAH
GENESIS CHAPTER 19: LOTS SALTY WIFE

My Dearest Bible Tea Sippers, remember how I told y'all God came with two angels to visit Abraham and Sarah to bless their old brittle selves with a child? Well, the angels left from their house to go straight to this messy, sinful city. They did *not* find ten righteous people. It's about to go down!

SO, BOOM WHAT HAD HAPPENED WAS...

The people of Sodom and Gomorrah were acting a hot mess, umm, kay. Lust was running rampant in the streets, chiile! By the time the angels arrived after leaving Abraham's house, it was nighttime. Lot was chilling at the gate of the city when he saw them. Immediately, he ran to them, bowed, and said, "What's up? Come chill at my house and let me treat y'all tonight, because it ain't safe in these streets!"

The angels were like, "Nah, we're good. We're just gonna sleep out here in the open plaza." Lot was like, "Absolutely not! Please come home with me!" So, the angels went home with Lot and enjoyed a meal. But before the angels could even lay their heads down to sleep, all the dudes, young and old, of the city came pounding on Lot's door! They were like, "Yooooo, Lotty, whose ya lil' fraannss you got up in there? Tell them to come out so we can sleep with 'em and show 'em a good time, not a long time." (Sips on tea with wide eyes!)

Lot went outside and saw that his whole house was surrounded! He tried his best to negotiate with these crusty, lusty men, but they were not listening. Lot said, "Listen, please don't do this. These men are under my protection in my house. In fact, I got two daughters that are virgins y'all can have instead. (Whhaat?!) But the mens dem was like, "Naaahh. First of all, you're just a visitor in our city. Second of all, you don't run nothing!" They started trying to break down the door!

Well, the angels had about enough of this crusty, lusty mustiness. They reached outside and snatched Lot right back in the house, then struck everybody outside with blindness! The angels said to Lot, "Gather up all ya people, 'cause we're about to make it rain on this city, and we ain't talking 'bout money! God has had enough with the wickedness in this city, so we've come to destroy it with sulfur and brimstone!"

So, Lot went to find his son-in laws, who were betrothed to his daughters for marriage. (They didn't seal the marriage yet; that's why his daughters were still virgins.) He tried to warn them to come with him because God was about to destroy the city, but they thought Lot was joking so they didn't go with him. (You can't say he didn't try.)

When the morning came, the angels woke Lot up and told him to get his wife and two daughters and run for their lives. Lot hesitated a little too long for the angels' liking. So, they grabbed everyone and ran with them to the city walls. One of the angels said, "Escape now! Run for your lives. Don't stop in the valley. Keep running until you get to the mountains of Moab. Remember this one thing, Do not look back!"

Lot tried to negotiate with the angels. He didn't want to go to the mountains, instead he wanted to go to a small town called Zoar. Finally, the angel said, "Fine. You can go to your lil town. Now hurry and don't look back!"

Lot and his family started running for their dear lives! As soon as Lot's foot reached Zoar, fire rained down from heaven! Bombs of brimstone and flaming sulfur demolished Sodom and Gomorrah. Now, Lot was running in the front, but his wife was behind him. Then, Lot's wife had thee nerve, thee audacity, *to look back*. (Sis, you had one job!) Immediately, she was turned into a pillar of salt! Now, she is just standing there for all eternity, stuck in her feelings, looking all salty. Literally!

Eventually, Lot and his daughters left Zoar because they were too scared to stay there. So, they went to the mountains to live in a cave. Lot is full of grief! He just lost his house, all his friends, and his wife all in one day. Now, these crusty, dusty, lusty daughters started plotting with each other. The older one was like, "Ommmggg, everybody is gone! There are no men left on the entire planet. How will we ever get some D and have some kids?" I couldn't make this up if I tried!

So, you would think they would devise a plan to scout the new land & look for men, right? Nope! These two chicks decided to get their father drunk then took turns each night, raping the poor, grief stricken, drunken, unconscious, non-consenting man. Their nasty plan actually worked. The two daughters both got pregnant. No wonder his name is Lot cuz this is *a lot* to unpack.

SIP ON THIS TEA: Here's some biblical context to sip on.

Remember Lot's Wife

Do not look back! Four small words that hold such a big meaning. Lot's wife was running toward her future but could not resist looking back at her past. Biblical scholars determined that the Hebrew word for "look back" isn't just a physical movement of looking over your shoulder. It means to pay attention to or consider. The amplified translation of verse 26 says, "But Lot's wife, from behind him, [foolishly, longingly] looked [back toward Sodom in an act of disobedience], and she became a pillar of salt."

Lot's wife didn't just take a peek at Sodom; she longed for it in her heart. How many times have we tried to cling to something or someone God is clearly telling us to let go of? Lot's wife being turned into a pillar of salt holds great significance. Throughout Genesis, our main characters have erected pillars or altars in places of immense importance as a reminder of their journey. Lot's wife turning into a pillar of salt symbolizes an erected memorial to *not look back*.

Lot's Daughters

Lot's decision to pitch his tent toward Sodom turned out to be a horrible decision! He flirted with the idea that he could be close to wickedness but not be affected by it. Welp! He messed around and found out the hard way. He married a woman who grew up in the wicked culture of Sodom and passed down that wickedness to their daughters. The two daughters gave birth to the Moabite and Ammonite people, who were shunned due to their practice of incest, and though related to the tribe of Israel, constantly fought against them and led them to worship false gods. All because Lot thought the grass was greener on the other side and chose to make his home close to Sodom!

But all is not lost, because generations later, a certain woman by the name of Ruth, who was a Moabite woman, married a man named Boaz. They had a son named Obed, who had a son named Jesse, who then had a son named King David! But that's tea for another day.

Chapter Thirteen
THE STORY OF ABRAHAM & ISSAC
GENESIS CHAPTER 21: ISSAC IS BORN

My Dearest Bible Tea Sippers, I need y'all to crack open y'all Bibles and sip on Genesis Chapter 20 by yourselves. Abraham done lied *again* about Sarah being his sister after she got tooketh *again* by another king! She has got to be the most beautiful senior citizen that has ever walked the earth to keep getting kidnapped, chiile. Anywho, it's important because Abraham made a covenant with that king and dug some wells, which will be important in the future. So go ahead, stop right here, and read it. (Sips on tea patiently waiting for you to get back.)

Ok did you read it? Good! So let me tell you what happened next.

SO, BOOM WHAT HAD HAPPENED WAS...

God kept His promise. Sure nuff, a year later Sarah gave birth to a son. Abraham was one hundred years old, and Sarah was ninety years old. Abraham circumcised the baby when he was eight days old, just like God instructed him to do. Sarah finally said, "God sure does have a sense of humor. He makes me laugh. Everyone is going to laugh with joy at our miracle." So, they named the baby Isaac, which means laughter. (That is too cute.) But there was just one little problem. Hagar and her son Ishmael were still up in Sarah's house. One day, she saw Ishmael teasing her son Isaac, and that was all she needed to solve this problem. She said to Abraham, "Get this maid and her son up outta my house! No maid's nappy-headed child is going to be an heir like my son Isaac." (Oop! Ok she didn't talk about his hair, but you know how dem Petty Bettys are.)

All this baby mama drama was stressing old-head Abraham out! He was not feeling this. He loved his son Ishmael. But God reminded him that his blessed descendants would be through Isaac, not Ishmael. Plus, God already blessed Ishmael too. So, Abraham woke up at the crack of dawn to kick his baby mama and his son out the house. We know he was an extraordinarily rich man, so there was no way he was going to leave them empty-handed. So, he wrapped up some bread, filled a water pouch, and sent them on their way. (Wayment, dat's it? Chiiilllle!)

Poor Hagar got lost in the wilderness, wandering around, wondering where to go. On top of that, all the water was gone! So, she sat Ishmael down next to a bush, and she went to the opposite side because she did not want to see him die. Hagar and Ishmael were crying their eyes out when suddenly an angel appeared. The angel said, "What's the matter, boo? Don't be scared! God heard the cries from the young boi. I'm gonna need you to Get up! Then I'm gonna need you to get your son up! Go hold his hand because God is going to make him a great nation!" Suddenly, God opened her eyes, and she saw a well! She filled her water pouch, made sure Ishmael got some, then she drank her water and went about her business. (Periodt!)

Chapter Fourteen
ABRAHAM'S SACRIFICE
GENESIS CHAPTER 22

SO, BOOM WHAT HAD HAPPENED WAS...

Let's do a quick recap. Abraham and Sarah waited 25 years to finally receive God's promise of having a baby. Abraham was 100 years old, and Sarah was 99 years old when God blessed them with Isaac. Well now, God was ready to test Abraham's faithfulness. (Sips tea loudly.) One day, God said, "Ok, so hear me out. Take your *only* son, who you *love* so much, go to the land of Moriah, then I'm gonna need you to offer him as a burnt sacrifice!" (Spits tea out in bewilderment.)

So, Abraham, with *no* hesitation, woke up early, grabbed his donkey, some wood, and two of his young boi, turned to his son Isaac, and was like, "Road triiip!" By the third day, Abraham could see the place God told him to go in the distance, so he told the young dudes to stay with the donkey and wait for them to both get back. Abraham made Isaac carry the wood while he grabbed the fire and a knife.

Isaac was like, "Umm, Pops? I see the wood and the fire but where's the lamb for the burnt offering?" (Bless his lil heart.) Abraham said, "God will provide the sacrifice." When they finally got to the spot, he built an altar, placed the wood, then tied up poor Isaac and placed him on the altar! He grabbed the knife, lifted it up ready to strike...(The suspense is killing me.)

But an angel appeared and was like, "Bruh! Don't you lay a finger on dat boy! Yo, you really are bout it bout it for God. You were willing to give up your beloved son for God." Suddenly, a ram appeared, stuck in some thorns, so Abraham killed it and made a burnt offering unto the Lord.

SIP ON THIS TEA: Here's some biblical context to sip on.

Abraham's Faith

There's a phrase that always haunts me, especially since I struggle with procrastination. The quote says, "Delayed obedience is still disobedience." Wheew, chiile! It snatches my edges bald every time. There is something powerful in Abraham's, no hesitation to God's request. He didn't ask any questions. He didn't try to negotiate with God like he did when he was trying to save Lot from Sodom's destruction. The Bible says he got up the next morning and went.

But there is another important part of this story I don't want you to miss. I need you to sip slowly on this. In verse 55, the amplified translation says: "Abraham said to his servants, 'Settle down and stay here with the donkey; the young man and I will go over there and worship [God], and we will come back to you."

It's the *we* for me. Abraham knew he was coming back down with his son. Think about God's covenant with him. Think about the promise that his descendants will come from Isaac. Many biblical scholars always explain that God tested Abraham's obedience, but I think God also wanted to test Abraham's belief in His promise. Abraham proved he was really bout it bout it for God. Will you still believe and be obedient to what God is telling you to do, even if it looks like you're about to lose everything?

The Sacrifice

My Dearest Bible Tea Sippers, you may be wondering why God would put Abraham through this ordeal. I promise you, everything God does is intentional. This is one of those Bible "aha" moments that still blows my mind. I need y'all to sip on this slowly, cuz it's hot. Biblical scholars say that Mount Moriah, the place where God instructed Abraham to take his *beloved* son and sacrifice him, is the same area of Calvary! Yes, that Calvary! Where 2,000 years later, God put His only *beloved* son, whom He *loved*, on the altar of the *cross*, as a sacrifice, to show how much He was bout it bout for you and me!

Through Abraham and Isaac's story it's easy to put ourselves in Abraham's shoes and understand the weight of what this sacrifice really meant. God wanted us to get a glimpse into what His sacrifice really meant. Unlike Abraham, there was no ram in the bush to spare His son's life. His only son, Jesus, was the sacrificial Lamb of God.

Chapter Fifteen
ISSAC GETS A BRIDE
GENESIS CHAPTER 24

My Dearest Bible Tea Sippers, you may be wondering; how will Isaac have all these descendants? Well, hunty Isaac was single and ready to mingle. Let's sip on exactly how he found his wife.

SO, BOOM WHAT HAD HAPPENED WAS...

Our beloved, bad and bougie biddy Sarah passed away at the age of 127. Abraham was given land and a cave where he could bury his wife and secured a burial ground for all his family. Abraham knew his time was coming too, so he met with his trusted servant Eliezer and devised a plan to find his son a good wife. He said to Eliezer, "Place your hand under my thigh and take this oath. You betta *not* let my son marry any of these Canaanite crusty women! Promise me you will travel back to the land of my fathers and find Isaac a wife from my kinfolk."

Eliezer swore the oath and promised not to take Isaac with him. If he didn't find a bride, then he just needed to come back, but under no circumstances was Isaac to leave the land that was destined to be his. So, our boy Eliezer left on this matchmaking journey with ten camels and loads of gifts. Now, Eliezer had no clue how he was supposed to find the perfect bride or even convince her to come back with him to meet her soon-to-be husband. This felt like an impossible task. As he entered the city, he stopped by a well and did the only thing he knew would work: he prayed.

> ***Eliezer's Prayer***
> *O Lord, God of my master, hear my plea.*
> *Grant me success, let Your kindness be.*
> *Here I stand beside this well,*
> *As city daughters come to draw and dwell.*
> *Let the one who offers me a drink,*
> *And waters my camels without a blink,*
> *Be the one You've chosen for Isaac's life,*
> *A sign of Your love, a faithful wife.*
> *By this I'll know Your grace extends,*
> *To my master Abraham, your faithful friend.*

Before Ez could even finish praying, a beautiful young lady came to the well with an empty jar on her shoulder. Her name was Rebekah. Ez ran to her and asked for some water. Bekah was so kind; she quickly gave him some water. And then, without asking, she said, "Hold up. I'll get some water for your camels too." Well, Ez was beside himself. Is this the answer to his prayer? He asked her, "Who's your daddy and dem? Can I stay with y'all for the night?" Bekah explained that her daddy's name was Bethuel, her grandmother was Milcah, and her granddaddy's name was Nahor. (As in Abraham's brother!)

Ez was too hype! He put rings and bracelets on her hands and started praise breaking right there! Bekah ran to tell her family. When her brother Laban saw all the bling on her arms, he came outside all hype. He wanted to see who this rich dude was and what he wanted. He was like, "Whatchu doing still standing out here, my friend? Please come inside and eat with us!"

Before they ate, Eliezer told them all the tea. He told them about the oath he took from Abraham and his impossible task of finding a wife for Isaac. Then he shared his specific prayer and how Bekah appeared out of nowhere and did exactly what he prayed for. He also told them exactly how wealthy Isaac was. (All Laban heard was, cha-ching!)

Once they heard all this, Laban was like, "Oh well, if this is from the Lord, how can we say no? Bekah is right here. You can take her and go." Ez was so happy! He did it! He kept his oath to Abraham. He had people bring in all the gifts he brought with him for Bekah and also laced up her mother and brother Laban. Once the morning came, he could finally head home with Isaac's new bride.

But when the morning came, Laban started backpedaling and trying some tricks. He started saying that maybe Bekah needed to stay for like a week or something and then she could go.

Ez was like, "Tricks are for kids. We're leaving just like we agreed upon!" Laban then tried another trick. He said, "Well, let's ask Bekah what she wants to do." So, they called Bekah in, and Laban asked if she wanted to leave with this man. Bekah was like, "Yup! I'm out." (You betta go get your rich husband sis!) Laban had no choice but to bless his sister and let her go. Eliezer took Bekah and headed back home.

Now, Isaac was in his field praying and getting his praise and worship on when he saw camels coming up the road. So, he started walking in their direction. At the same time, Bekah saw this fine man walking in the fields coming their way.

Bekah said to Eliezer, "Um, who dat?" Ez was like, "Oh, that's him, my master Isaac." Bekah hopped off her camel so fast and put on the customary veil.

Now, Isaac was away this whole time and had no idea about all of Abraham and Ez's shenanigans to find him a wife. Ez ran down the whole story to him. Isaac wasted no time. He took his beautiful new cuzzo bride straight to his mother's tent and made her his wife. He was so in love, his broken heart finally healed from losing his beautiful mother, Sarah.

SIP ON THIS TEA: Here's some biblical context to sip on.

Sarah's Tent

Sarah was the Madam Mistress of the entire household. It was customary during these times that she would have her own tent. When she passed away, her tent would remain empty until a new mistress of the household took over. When Isaac took his new bride into his mother's tent, he was establishing that Rebekah was taking her rightful place as the new household's mistress.

Laban's Role

It is customary for the bride's father to do all the negotiating. Biblical scholars believe Laban took this role because his father was too old and frail to do so. Laban's immediate excitement was based on the wealth Eliezer presented. Remember, he traveled with ten camels carrying gifts. That is a huge bride dowry.

At first, his backpedaling may seem like just a protective brother trying to do what's best for his little sis. But we will soon learn that Laban is a liar, cheater, deceiver, and heartbreaker. But that's tea for another day.

Chapter Sixteen
THE STORY OF JACOB & ESAU
GENESIS CHAPTER 25: THE TWINS

Remember how I told y'all about Issac finding his wife Rebekah? Well, we're about to sip on all the drama of their kids Jacob and Esau.

SO, BOOM WHAT HAD HAPPENED WAS...

Isaac and Rebekah got married when Isaac was about forty years old. Unfortunately, she was having trouble getting pregnant, so Isaac prayed to the Lord. God granted his prayer, and Rebekah got pregnant with twin boys. Now, these two boys started fighting with each other from the time they were in their mama's womb! They were kicking and shoving each other until Rebekah couldn't take it anymore. So, she went to God to find out what was going on.

The Lord said to her, "Two nations are in your womb, and the separation of two nations has started within you. One nation is going to be stronger than the other, and the older is going to serve the younger."

When it was time to give birth, sure enough, they were twins! The first baby came out with all this reddish hair, looking like Chewbacca, so they named him Esau, which means "hairy." When the other baby came out, his hand was holding on to Esau's heel, so they named him Jacob, which means "one who grabs by the heel or supplanter."

Now, Esau's Chewbacca-looking self was a woodsy kind of dude. He loved to hunt and be out in the streets all day, while Jacob was a preppy, peaceful mama's boy that loved to stay home and whip up meals.

Isaac's favorite was Esau, but Rebekah's favorite was Jacob. (There goes that favoritism!) Traditionally, Esau came out first, so he was considered the firstborn; therefore, the birthright, inheritance, and blessings passed down from Abraham would go to him.

One day, Esau was in the streets all day, and he was starving like Marvin! Jacob was doing what he always did—cooking some stew. Esau said, "Gimme some of that stew, I'm exhausted and famished!" So, Jacob, with his supplanter self, said, "I'll give you some, but first you gotta give me your first-born birthright."

Esau was so hungry, he said, "What good is a birthright if I die from hunger?" So, Jacob made him swear an oath, and Esau sold him his birthright for some red stew! From that day on, Esau was salty and scorned his birthright.

SIP ON THIS TEA: Here's some biblical context to sip on.

Jacob's Name Deeper Meaning

According to Reverend Merriam Webster, that's the dictionary, y'all, to "supplant" means to supersede another, especially by force or treachery. Jacob's name may have come about because he was physically holding on to Esau's heel; however, he lived up to his name with all his treacherous trickery. Treachery will follow him and cause him lots of heartache, not only through his own trickery but as a generational pattern repeated through his children.

Chapter Seventeen
ISSAC & THE KING
Genesis Chapter 26

You might be thinking, how did we get here? What happened to Jacob and Esau? Why are we talking about their daddy Isaac? Well, this entire family is full of drama and dysfunction. It's important to point out all the repeated toxic patterns in their bloodline. Don't worry, My Dear Bible Tea Sippers. Trust me, it all connects! Nothing is random with God.

SO, BOOM WHAT HAD HAPPENED WAS...

There was a famine in the land, so Isaac moved to Gerar. This land was ruled by King Abimelech, king of the Philistines. God appeared to him and said, "Don't go to Egypt! Stay where I tell you to stay. I need you to lay low and blend in just for a lil bit. I will be with you and bless you. I made an oath with your daddy Abraham, so I'll make that oath with you. All of these lands will be yours and your descendants. Your descendants will multiply like the stars in the sky. Your pops listened, obeyed my voice, and kept my laws; because of this, all the nations on the earth will be blessed!"

One day, the men of Gerar asked Isaac about his wife Rebekah. Isaac lied and said she was his sister because he was scared they would kill him and take her because she was a baddie! (Sound familiar?) After they had been there for a while, one day King Abimelech looked out his window and saw Isaac rubbing up on Rebekah all hot and heavy! The King was like, "Hold up! Wait a minute! That is not your sister! Why you be lying?!"

Isaac explained his reasoning, but King Abimelech wasn't having it! He was mad because any one of the men could have taken advantage of Rebekah, thinking she wasn't married, and brought guilt on the entire land. So, the king declared that if anyone touched Rebekah, they would be put to death!

Now, with his wife protected, Isaac started setting up shop. He got in his farmer's bag and started planting seeds. In the same year, he reaped one hundred times more than what he planted. The Lord blessed and favored him. Isaac was blessed and bougie! He became very wealthy, and everybody knew he was that boy!

So here come the haters. The Philistines were so jealous. They filled up all the wells that Abraham dug back in the day with dirt! (They did him dirty. Literally!) Even King Abimelech turned on him. The king was like, "You got to go! You've become way too powerful." So, Isaac left that region and set up camp in the Valley of Gerar.

Now, this is where this tea starts to get hot and petty! So, Isaac moved to the valley and reopened the wells that belonged to Abraham that were now mysteriously filled with dirt. But when his servants dug in the wells and the water sprung out, all of a sudden, here come the herdsmen of Gerar talking about that's their water!! (Um what?) So, Isaac named that well Esek, which means "quarreling."

His herdsmen moved and dug out another well, and sure enough, those petty bettys came running, talking about that's their water too! Isaac named that well "Sitnah," which means enmity. When they dug the next well, there was no drama, so Isaac pitched a tent and built an altar after having an encounter with God. Eventually, Isaac and King Abimelech came to a truce and created a covenant with one another. You can sip on how their story ends for yourself in Genesis Chapter 26.

SIP ON THIS TEA: Here's some biblical context to sip on.

Abraham's Dysfunctional Patterns

Father Abraham had many sons, but he also had a lot of dysfunctional patterns that he passed down to his children. In Genesis 12 and 20, Abraham lies on two separate occasions about Sarah being his sister. His son Isaac then lies to King Abimelech, (Most likely a different King with the same title in Genesis 20, kinda like how Pharoah and Caesar are titles for different rulers.) about Rebekah being his wife for the same reason as Abraham. Lying is a generational pattern this family is plagued with, as we soon will witness as we sip on Jacob's Bible Tea.

Naming of the Wells

If naming these wells "quarrel" and "enmity" ain't foreshadowing to what is in store for Isaac's family, then I don't know what is! Isaac and Ishmael were pitted against each other from the jump with Abraham's baby mama drama with Sarah and Hagar. We just learned that Jacob and Esau were warring with each other from the womb. Biblical scholars believe the conflict that arises in this family is a deep representation of the conflict between God's people and those outside of his covenant. A raging conflict that is still happening today in modern times.

Chapter Eighteen
TREACHEROUS TRICKERY
GENESIS CHAPTER 27

Remember the meaning of Jacob's name? Wheeww chiile! We're about to learn exactly why Jacob ain't nothing but a treacherous trickster.

SO, BOOM WHAT HAD HAPPENED WAS...

At this point in our story, Isaac is a blind old geezer. He knew his time was coming to an end; he just didn't know when. So, he called his favorite son Esau to him. He told him, "Son, I'm old and I don't know when I'm going to die. I want to bless you before I go. Take your hunting gear, go catch me some good game, and make me some of that soup that I love so much.

Now, Bekah's trickery self was ear hustling and overheard what Isaac said. So, she went to her favorite son, Jacob, and said, "Listen to me carefully! I just heard your father say he's about to give his blessings to your brother! But I got a plan; follow my directions to the T. Go get me two young goats so I can make your father's favorite stew, and I'm going to have you bring it to him instead of Esau."

But Jacob was like, "Um, mama, I'm a smooth brotha. I'm not hairy like Esau! As soon as pops touches me and doesn't feel that Chewbacca fur, he's going to curse me instead of bless me." Bekah responded, "If that happens, let that curse be on me. Now do as I say."

Jacob got the two goats so Bekah could kill them and prepare the soup. Then, her trickery self took Esau's clothes, put them on Jacob, then took the skins of the two goats and put them on his hands and his neck. Jacob greeted Isaac as he brought the stew to him. Isaac immediately was like, "Who dat?" Jacob replied, "It's me, your firstborn son, Esau! I did what you asked me to do. Please sit up so you can eat some of this good stew."

Isaac was like, "How did you hunt so fast, son?" Jacob, lying self, said, "Because your God caused the game to come to me. (Instant side eye!) Isaac wasn't feeling it, so he said, "Come closer so I can lay hands on you and see if you're really my boy Esau."

When the supplanter came closer, Isaac touched his hands and felt how hairy they were. "Well, you sound like my son Jacob, but you definitely feel like my Esau." Isaac asked, "Are you really my son Esau? Bring me my food so that I may bless you." When he was done eating, he asked his son for a kiss. When Jacob kissed him, Isaac said, "You definitely smell like outside; you must be Esau."

So poor deceived Isaac gave Jacob the following blessing:

Jacob's Blessing
The scent of my son—pure, rich, divine,
Like fields anointed by God's own design.
May the heavens break open, let the dew descend,
God's hand in the rain, making droughts rescind.
May the earth stretch wide, obey His command,
Grain in your storehouse, wine in your hand.

May men bow in service, nations speak your name,
Honor etched deep, like stone carved in flame.
You will rise as Lord, your brothers will see,
Not by your will, but divine decree.
And know this—who dares to curse your path,
Will taste the weight of a wrath that lasts.
But those who bless, who lift your name,
Will drink from wells that never drain.

(Bars!)

Now, as soon as Isaac was done dropping the mic, Jacob skedaddled up out of there. He got away just in the nick of time because Esau was coming with his bowl of stew. When he brought it to his father, he was all hype and said, "Hey, Pops, sit up and get you some of this good stew, and then let me get that blessing!" Isaac was like, "Ehh what? Who dat?!" all confused and senile! (Sips tea loudly.) Esau said, "It's me, pops, Esau, your first-born son."

Chiile, Isaac was so shooketh! He said trembling, "Then who was just here? I already ate soup and blessed him with your blessing, and I can't take the blessing back!" When Esau heard this, he let out a blood-curdling cry! "Bless me too, father!" he cried. (Poor Chewbacca!) But Isaac told him that Jacob already deceitfully took his blessing.

Esau was distraught. He said, "Y'all named him the right thang because he supplanted me twice. First, when he took my birthright and now when he stole my blessing! You can't only have one blessing? You gotta bless me too!" Isaac explained that he made Jacob his master and gave all his brothers to him as servants. This made Esau cry even harder, so Isaac blessed him with these bars:

Esau's Blessing

Your dwelling—far from the earth's embrace,
Far from the heavens, no favor, no grace.
The soil won't yield, the rain won't fall,
You'll walk through drought, you'll taste it all.
You'll live by the sword, steel in your hand,
Fighting for breath, fighting for land.
Serving your brother, bowing low,
Bound by a yoke that grinds your soul.
But hear me now—there comes a day,
When rage and chains will fall away.
When the fire inside breaks through the pain,
And you rise up, unshackled, untamed.
The weight will lift, the yoke will snap,
And freedom will call—ain't no turning back.

From then on, Esau hated Jacob and vowed that when his Pops died, he was going to kill Jacob on sight! When Bekah heard what Esau was planning, she told Jacob to, "run, Forrest, run!" She told Jacob it was time to stop being a mama's boy. She gave him instructions to escape to her brother Laban in the land of Haran. She promised when his brother's anger dwindled and he forgot about what Jacob did to him, she would send for him to come back home.

Isaac warned Jacob to never marry a Canaanite woman. Instead, he should marry one of Laban's daughters. So, Jacob left and started his journey to Uncle Laban's. He thought he was leaving all the destruction from his trickery behind. Little did he know that treacherous trickery was waiting to give him a taste of his own medicine.

SIP ON THIS TEA: Here's some biblical context to sip on.

Esau's Birthright

In ancient Hebrew families, a birthright was an honor reserved for the firstborn son. It usually included a double portion of the father's property and possessions. The eldest son also received the father's most extravagant blessing. Biblically, the blessing was a prophetic statement the father speaks through the guidance of the Holy Spirit. The birthright and blessing functioned as the family patriarch's last will and testament.

As much as we want to sympathize with Esau, let's not be fooled or blinded by empathy. He gave up his birthright for a bowl of soup, chiile! It's easy to be moved by his sobbing and complete emotional breakdown. But Esau completely disregarded the spiritual significance of his rightful place. He was willing to give up his spiritual position for a temporary possession.

Umm, now that will preach!

I want you to take a moment to take your teaspoon and slowly sip on Hebrews 12: 15-17. The Message Translation says it like this:

> Watch out for the Esau syndrome: trading away God's lifelong gift in order to satisfy a short-term appetite. You well know how Esau later regretted that impulsive act and wanted God's blessing—but by then it was too late, tears or no tears. ~ MSG

Esau's Blessing

Although it's easy to blame Rebekah for scheming Esau out of his blessing, let's take a deeper look at Isaac. It was already prophesied that, "the older will serve the younger," yet Isaac let favoritism blind him to God's will.

Isaac was shooketh when he discovered he really gave the blessing to Jacob, who God intended for it to go to anyway! God intended for Jacob to be the chosen one to inherit the covenant God made with Abraham. Although Jacob's name meant supplanter, eventually his name would be changed to Israel, and his children would lay the foundation for the nation of God's chosen people. Isaac tried to give his blessing to Esau despite what the prophecy said but Rebekah's schemes fulfilled God's prophecy anyway.

Esau's blessing may sound more like a curse, but there is an immense blessing in it for all of us. Isaac prophesied that Esau would live by the sword and serve his brother; however, when he finally let go of his hatred and anger, he would finally be free of that chokehold. How many of us are enslaved to our hatred and anger and can't access our blessings because we refuse to let them go? But that's another whole teapot for another day!

Chapter Nineteen
THE STORY OF JACOB, RACHEL & LEAH
GENESIS CHAPTER 28: JACOB'S SISTER WIVES

Remember how Jacob had to run away because he tricked his father and stole his twin brother's blessing? Welp! He's about to mess around and find out what it feels like to get tricked!

SO, BOOM WHAT HAD HAPPENED WAS...

Jacob left his mama's house and traveled to Haran to find his uncle, Laban. On one particular night he decided to set up camp and take it down for the night since it was getting dark. He used a stone for a pillow and started to drift asleep.

He had a life-changing dream. In his vision, he saw a gigantic ladder that stretched from earth all the way to the heavens. There were angels coming up and down the ladder. At the very top, he saw God!

The Lord said to him:

Jacob's Ladder Prophecy
I am the Lord—the Ancient Name,
The God of Abraham, Isaac the same.
This land you rest on, this ground you claim,

It's yours, your children—forever unchanged.
And through your name, through your seed,
Nations will rise, the world will be freed.
Every tribe, every tongue, every place on this earth,
Will feel the weight of your promise, your worth.
Behold—I am with you, I walk by your side,
A shield in the storm, a light that can't hide.
Wherever you go, My hand will stay,
Keeping you close, never astray.
Your bloodline?
Like dust, too vast to see,
Carried by winds, yet rooted in Me.
Stretching west, reaching east,
Spreading north and south—never ceased.
Through you, the nations will rise and be blessed,
A promise sealed, a name professed.
And I am with you, wherever you go,
My hand will guide, My presence will show.
And when the time comes, when the journey is through,
I'll bring you back—what I said, I will do.
I do not leave, I do not break,
What I have spoken, no man can take.

Jacob woke up from his dream and realized he had laid down in a special place and didn't even realize it. He said to himself, "There is no place like this! This must be the gateway to heaven!" The next morning, Jacob took the same stone he used as a pillow, gathered more stones, and made a pillar. He poured olive oil over it to consecrate it, and he named that very spot Bethel, which means "The House of God."

Jacob decided to make a vow to God. He said:

Jacob's Vow
If God roll with me, keep me strong,
Walk this path, keep me movin' on.
If He feed my soul, keep my fit right,
Cover my steps when I move through the night.
If He bring me back, no scratch, no harm,
Safe to my father's,
wrapped in His arms— Then He's my God,
I'm going all out.
The One I trust, no diggity, no doubt!

Jacob continued his journey to the land of the East. He pulled up to a field with shepherds and their flocks of sheep. He asked the good brothers where they were from, and they said Haran! When Jacob asked if they knew his Unc Laban, they said Laban was doing well, and in fact, his daughter Rachel was on her way with his flock to drink from the well.

When Jacob saw the beautiful Rachel making her way, he removed the heavy stone that covered the well. He gave water to all of her flock and then grabbed her and began crying. He kissed her and told her that he was Jacob, Rebekah's son. Rachel ran to tell her father that his nephew had traveled all the way to find him.

As soon as Laban heard about his nephew, he ran to meet him. Laban invited Jacob to come home with them. Jacob told his uncle everything that happened. Laban reassured him that he was his flesh and bone, and he was safe to stay with them. After some time, Laban told Jacob that just because he was his relative, that didn't mean he should work for free. Laban asked Jacob what he wanted his wages to be. Now Laban had two daughters. Rachel was gorgeous; she was a straight baddie!

Leah on the other hand was just bad-looking. OK, technically it says she had weak eyes. I don't know if that meant she had weak lazy eyes that was wandering all over the place or when you looked at her it made your eyes weak either way, she didn't look like Rachel um kaaayy!

Jacob was madly in love with Rachel, so he decided to tell Uncle Laban that he would work for him for seven years just to have the privilege of marrying her. Laban agreed because he figured it was better to give her to Jacob instead of some stranger. So, Jacob worked seven long years, dreaming of the day he could finally marry his beautiful bride.

Fast forward seven years later, Jacob was all hyped and told Laban he was ready for his bride! So, Laban got everybody together for a wedding feast with lots of wine. But that night, Laban took Leah to Jacob's room, not Rachel! When Jacob came in, he immediately laid with her and consummated the marriage. In the morning, Jacob rolled over and realized it was Leah's weak-eyed self staring back at him! He was pissed! He said to Laban, "How could you do this to me?! I worked seven long years for you just so I could marry Rachel! Why would you lie to me and trick me into marrying Leah!" (Sips tea loudly.)

But Laban explained, "Look nephew, it's against tradition for the younger daughter to be given away in marriage before the oldest daughter. The younger can't take the tradition before the oldest. Finally, Laban made a compromise. He told Jacob to finish out the week-long wedding celebration with Leah and he would also give him Rachel, but Jacob would need to work an additional seven years. Jacob agreed. He finished the week with Leah, and Laban gave him Rachel as his second wife. However, Jacob lived with Rachel and loved her more than Leah. God saw how Leah was not loved! He blessed her with the ability to have children, but Jacob's favorite wife, Rachel, was barren.

Now, fast-forward a little. Every time Leah popped a baby out, she started naming them names to represent how she was feeling. With her first-born son, she said, "The Lord sees my humiliation, so He gave me a son. Now my husband will love me. So, I'm going to name him Reuben, which means 'See, a son.'" Then she had another son and said, "Because God hears that I am unloved, I am going to name him Simeon, which means 'God hears.'"

When she had her third son, she said, "Now my husband is going to become attached to me because I gave him three sons. So, I am going to name him Levi, which means 'joined and united.'" When she had her fourth son, she said, "Praise the Lord, Won't He do it!" So, she named him Judah, which means "praise and thanksgiving." But then, all of a sudden, she couldn't get pregnant again.

Rachel had enough! She couldn't stand the fact that ugly-behind Leah got to have all the babies with her man! She said to Jacob, "Give me kids or I'm finna die!" Jacob was like, "What I look like, God?" Rachel was like, "You know what, take my maid Bilhah. I want you to get her pregnant, and then when she gives birth, she'll sit on my knees, and that way her kids will be my kids." (What in the Handmaid's Tale?! It's giving Sarah and Hagar!)

So, Jacob took Bilhah as a secondary wife. When she gave birth to a son, Rachel said, "God judged my pain and heard my prayers." So, she named him Dan, which means "He judged." Bilhah popped out another son; this time Rachel said, "I fought with my sister and won!" So, she named him Naphtali, which means "my wrestling."

Now, when Leah saw with her weak eyes that she couldn't have any more children, she decided to take her maid Zilpah and give her to Jacob as a secondary wife too. (I couldn't make this up if I tried.) When Zilpah gave birth to a son, Leah decided to join in the petty name-giving and said, "Would you look at that, how fortunate for me!" So, she named him Gad, which means "good fortune." Zilpah had another son, and Leah said, "Chiile, I'm so happy! I'm so happy that all the women will start calling me happy as my new name!" So, she named the baby Asher, which means "happy."

One day, Leah's son Reuben went to the field and brought home some mandrakes for his mother. When Rachel saw them, she was like, "Hey, sis! Heyyy. Can I please have some of those mandrakes?" Leah was like, "Oh, you already took my husband, now you want to take my son's mandrakes too?" So, Rachel said, "You know what? How about this, in exchange for the mandrakes, Jacob can sleep with you tonight." (Jesus wept.)

That night, as Jacob was making his way home from the fields, Leah popped out at him and was like, "Aht aht, you ain't going home tonight! You're coming with me because I bought you for the night!" Welp! Leah got pregnant that night! She gave birth to a son and named him Issachar, which means "my reward."

Leah then gave birth *again* to her sixth son. She said, "Oh, this must be a good marriage gift. Now, Jacob will live with me and give me the honor as his wife because I now gave him six sons." So, she named him Zebulun, which means "to dwell with." Then Leah gave birth to a daughter and named her Dinah, which means "judgment."

Finally, after all these years, God blessed Rachel. When she gave birth, she said, "God finally took away my humiliation and disgrace." The baby was Jacob's favorite son because it was the child he finally had with the wife he genuinely loved. The baby's name means "May God give me more." His name was Joseph.

SIP ON THIS TEA: Here's some biblical context to sip on.

Biblical scholars have argued for centuries on exactly what the Bible meant when it said, "Leah had weak eyes." The Hebrew word, "Rakkot," can be translated to tender or delicate, which in modern times would be interpreted as she was pretty with soft eyes. But in ancient times, tender and delicate were not associated with attractive features. They were not characteristics that were marriage material. The verse actually says, "Leah had weak eyes, but Rachel was beautiful in form and appearance." (Gen 29:17 AMP)

That conjunction word, "but," can't be ignored. The verse is saying, in contrast to what Leah looked like, Rachel was beautiful not only in her character and how she presented herself, but also in her physical appearance.

In all honesty, having weak eyes could have meant Leah was just a plain Jane and kind of boring. Regardless of her appearance, she was unloved, and God saw her pain. God still loved her, regardless of how Jacob felt toward her.

Wedding Feast

The first question that comes to mind is: how in the world did Jacob not recognize that he was with Leah and not Rachel? Well, in ancient times, a wedding ceremony was not how it is today. The feast that Laban had the first night was a drunken celebration for all his men. No women would have been present because this was not actually the wedding ceremony, which means Jacob may have been intoxicated and waiting in the dark for Laban to bring him his bride. Traditionally, the bride would have entered with her face covered with a veil. I think it's safe to say there wasn't any talking going on that night.

Cultural Traditions

It's important to note Laban's insistence on honoring his cultural traditions. Traditionally, he could not give Leah away for marriage first because she was not the firstborn. Just like Esau was the firstborn son, so traditionally, he was supposed to have the birthright and the blessing from Isaac. It's so ironic that Jacob was tricked by someone who honored this tradition when he tricked his father into dishonoring the tradition by stealing Esau's blessing.

Mandrakes

Mandrakes are part of the nightshade plant family. In ancient times, they had both poisonous and medicinal uses. They ranged from being used as anesthetics, narcotics, hallucinogens, sedatives, and even laxatives. They could have also been used to help with fertility. It's important to note that even though Leah tried to take it into her own hands to get pregnant again, it was Rachel who traded Jacob for the mandrakes. Jacob slept with Leah that night, and the Bible specifically says God opened Leah's womb.

The Irony

Let's take a moment to take a long sip on the irony of the trickster getting tricked.

- Isaac was blind and could not tell the difference between Jacob and Esau.

- Jacob was in the dark and could not tell the difference between Leah and Rachel.

- Isaac wants his blessing to go to his favorite son but gets tricked into giving it to his other son.

- Jacob wants to marry his favorite out of Laban's daughters but gets tricked into marrying his other daughter.

- Issac's servant took Rebekah away from Laban so she can marry Isaac even though Laban wanted his sister to stay a little longer.

- Laban turns around and takes Isaac's son and makes him stay longer than what was agreed upon.

Ohhh the irony!

Chapter Twenty
Lying Laban
Genesis Chapter 30

My Dearest Bible Tea Sippers, you may be thinking that surely the trickster Jacob has now had a taste of his own medicine and now he will live in peace. Unfortunately, lying behind Laban was not through with our boy yet. As the saying goes, "If one is to be called a liar, one may as well make an effort to deserve the name."

SO, BOOM WHAT HAD HAPPENED WAS...

After Rachel had Joseph, Jacob felt that it was about time to head out. He said to Laban, "I'm ready to go back home. I've worked extremely hard for you, so please grant me my release. Give me my wives and children, so we can go."

Laban was like, "Hold up, nephew—I mean son-in-law. Look, I've learned that I have been prosperous because of you and your God. Y'all can't leave yet. Name your price, and I'll pay you to stay."

Jacob was like, "You don't gotta pay me anything. It's time for me to take care of my own family. How about this: When I leave, I'll take any newborn animals that are speckled, spotted, or all black as my share. When it's time for me to go, I'll take all that belongs to me with me, and if you find any that don't have a speck or spot on them, you will know that I stole them from you."

Lying behind, Laban said, "It's a deal!" But he was lying. He went to the rest of his flock and took out every black, spotted, and speckled animal and gave them to his sons, leaving Jacob with the rest. Then he left and put a three-day's journey of distance between him and Jacob.

So, Jacob was left with a bunch of white lambs and black goats. How in the world would they produce speckled or spotted offspring? No worries! That was light work for Jacob and his God. Jacob got in his farmer's bag and did some unconventional farming techniques, and God blessed those animals with miraculous streaked, spotted, and speckled offspring. Six years later, Jacob's flocks grew so much he became rich! He even had his own servants, camels, and donkeys. He was prosperous throughout the land, and everyone knew he was that boy!

Of course, you already know what's about to happen whenever someone starts doing well—here come dem haters! Jacob started hearing Laban's sons talking about him. They were saying that he was too rich and took everything away from Laban. He even noticed that Laban had a little stinking attitude toward him too. Finally, God said to Jacob, "It's time to go! Return to the land of your Father. I will be with you."

So, Jacob called his wives to him and was like, "Look, I served y'all father for an extraordinarily long time. He's done nothing but lie and try to cheat me. But the God of my father was always with me. If Laban said, 'Oh, now you can only have all the spotted offspring,' miraculously, only spotted offspring would be born. Then he would change it and be like, 'Oh, you can only have the speckled offspring,' and once again, miraculously, only speckled animals would be born. Clearly, God is with me, and it's time to go!"

Rachel and Leah agreed because they felt that Laban was treating them bad too. All he wanted was money, and that's all he really ever cared about. They finally agreed on something and told Jacob, "Let's do what God is telling you to do!" So while Laban was away shearing his sheep, Jacob snuck out with all of his family, his servants, and all of his livestock. But before they left, Rachel stole one of her father's household god statues out of spite because she wanted an inheritance. (No ma'am!)

When Laban got back home and found out they left, he took his people with him and pursued them for seven whole days until he caught up to them! Laban confronted Jacob. He was like, "Why'd you leave like that? Why you sneaking off and taking my daughters like you kidnapped them or something? Why you ain't even let me kiss my grandkids goodbye? You being all sneaky and stuff! If you would have told me, I would have sent you off with a going-away party. What you did is disrespectful! I have every right to hurt you right now. But that God of yours appeared to me in a dream and told me to be careful how I speak to you. That's fine or whatever. You must be homesick, so I'll let you go. However, you stole my household god, so I'm gonna need that back now!"

Jacob was like, "I left secretly because I was afraid you would take your daughters from me by force. I don't got nothing to hide! So, if you find your household god in any of my things, the person who took it will be put to death." Little did Jacob know that it was his favorite wifey Rachel who had the sticky fingers. (Yikkessss!)

So, Laban searched everybody's tent, but he couldn't find his idol. Finally, he got to Rachel's tent. Rachel hid the idol in one of the camel bags and was sitting on it when her father entered. He was searching all over the tent but couldn't find it. Rachel finally said, "Please excuse me, father. Please don't be angry; I didn't get up and greet you when you came in. I'm on my period, and I'm feeling too sick to stand up." (Girl!) Laban kept searching, but he didn't find it.

Finally, Jacob had enough! He argued with Laban and said, "I'm done! It's not my fault you're missing your little god thingy. I've been with you for twenty years, and I'm sick and tired of these games! First, I worked fourteen years just to marry your daughters. Then I had to work six years to gain my own wealth to leave, and you changed my wages ten times! No matter what you did to me, God was with me, and clearly, he has never left me. God saw my humiliation and how tired I am of everything you've done to me, and that's why he spoke to you in a dream!"

Lying behind Laban decided to end all his lies. He made a covenant with Jacob to cause no more harm and tried to swear an oath to God and his little false god too, but Jacob wasn't having that. He only swore his oath to the God of his father, Isaac, and his grandfather, Abraham. He declared that The Lord was his only God, no diggity, no doubt.

SIP ON THIS TEA: Here are some personal reflections to sip on.

What's your T.E.A.? Thoughts. Emotions. Actions.

Jacob stayed in Laban's mess *way* too long. Sometimes we get so used to dysfunction, we start calling it normal. The filth stops stinking, and we forget what freedom even feels like.

But comfort isn't the same as calling. God will always give you the courage to leave what no longer honors Him—or you.

My Dearest Bible Tea Sippers, is it time to go?

Journal your T.E.A.—check your *Thoughts,* name your *Emotions,* and take *Action* that moves you toward freedom, not fear.

Chapter Twenty-One
THE STORY OF JACOB & ESAU'S REUNION
GENESIS CHAPTER 30: JACOB'S FEAR

Remember how the last time we heard from Esau; he was going to kill Jacob on sight?! Welp! These two brothers are about to meet face to face!

SO, BOOM WHAT HAD HAPPENED WAS…

Jacob, along with Rachel, Leah, their children, and all of his secondary wives finally left Laban's household behind and began the journey back home. On the way, an angel met with Jacob to encourage him that everything was going to be alright.

Jacob decided to send messengers ahead of him to bring a message to his brother Esau in the land of Seir. The messages said:

> **Jacob's Message**
> *It's ya servant Jacob—remember me?*
> *Been out with Laban, just tryin' be free.*
> *Years done passed, but now I stand,*
> *With flocks and herds, blessed by His hand.*
> *Oxen, donkeys, wealth increased,*
> *Servants galore, my house got peace.*

But I send this word, not to boast, not to fight,
Just to find grace, to make things right.

When the messengers returned, they only had this to say:

The Message
We spoke to Esau, gave him your message,
But now he's coming—no time for leverage.
Four hundred deep, no words were said,
Marchin' this way, eyes fixed ahead.

Chiile, Jacob was shooketh! Esau didn't send a message back instead he was on his way with 400 men! Jacob came up with a plan. He divided the people that were with him into two groups. He decided that if Esau attacked one of the groups, at least the other group could escape to safety.

Then Jacob prayed.

Jacob's Prayer
O God— the God of my father's past,
Abraham walked with You, Isaac held fast.
You told me, "Go back to your land, your kin,"
Said You'd prosper me, Lord—said You'd bring me in.
But who am I? Unworthy, small,
Yet Your grace still caught me, didn't let me fall.
I had nothing but a staff in my hand,
Crossed that Jordan, now look where I stand!
Two camps strong—blessed beyond sight,
But now I'm facing a war I can't fight.

Save me! Lord, I'm crying out loud,
Esau is coming, four hundred proud.
I fear, Lord—he might strike, might kill,
The mothers, the children, blood might spill.
But You, Lord—You made a vow!
Said You'd bless my seed, can't stop it now!
As countless as sand, beyond the sea,
You spoke it, Lord—so let it be!

(Whew! That's a desperate prayer!)

Jacob needed another plan fast. He decided that he was going to take a whole bunch of his flock and gift them to Esau. But first, he had to be all extra about how he was going to present them to his twin. The plan was to separate the flock into herds, and then, as each herd got to Esau, the servant would say, "All of these are your servant Jacob's. They are a gift for his brother Esau. He is also coming behind us."

Jacob thought that at least by the time he actually got to Esau, all of the gifts would soften him up and make him forgive him. Jacob made the plan, but he was still scared. So, in the middle of the night, he got up, took all his wives and eleven children, and sent them to wait across a brook.

Jacob was left all alone. But not for long.

Chapter Twenty-Two
Jacob Wrestles
Genesis Chapter 32

───◆○◆───

My Dearest Bible Tea Sippers, the last time we spoke that treacherous trickster Jacob was all by himself in the middle of the night with the looming threat of his twin brother Esau, marching towards him with four hundred of his homies! I'm so sorry to leave you on such a cliffhanger, but I must stop here so I can tell you that Jacob is about to get into the fight of his life but it ain't with Esau, hunty!

SO, BOOM WHAT HAD HAPPENED WAS...

It's the middle of the night. Jacob is all by himself in the dark when suddenly a man appears. Out of nowhere the man and Jacob start wrestling! I'm talking bout they are out there in the middle of the wilderness, straight tussling! The fight is so long that the sun is starting to come up!

When the man saw that Jacob wasn't giving up, he reached down, touched Jacob's hip, and the whole thang popped out of its socket. (Ouch!) The man finally said, "Yo! Let me go! The day is coming!" but Jacob replied, "I am not letting you go until you bless me!" The man asked, "What's your name?" The supplanter answered him and said, "My name is Jacob." The man replied, "From now on your name shall no longer be called Jacob, but Israel. Because you wrestled with God and with man and you have prevailed.* Jacob tried to ask the man what his name was, but the man was like, "Why you asking me questions?," declared a blessing on Jacob, and then, poof! He left.

SIP ON THIS TEA: Here's some biblical context to sip on.

The Stranger

Biblical scholars say that the mysterious man appears to be God himself or an angel in a man's form. Do you remember what it's called when God makes appearances like this? Go ahead and flip back and sip on that tea again so you can remember. Come on back when you're ready. I'll wait for you.

Let's keep sipping...

When the man supernaturally injures Jacob, he finally realizes that this is no ordinary man! Jacob uses this opportunity to finally fight for his own blessing. Not steal it or trick his way into getting it. Nope! Not this time. This time, he painstakingly fights for his life to get his own blessing. He refused to let go until God blessed him.

Jacob's Name Change

In order to get the blessing God demands Jacob to identify himself. Jacob's name literally means supplanter. According to the great minister Google, (Yes, the search engine.) "supplanter" can also be translated to mean: one who wrongfully or illegally seizes and holds the place of another.

The Hebrew translation of Jacob's name means, "to seize the heel or figuratively to trip up or deceive." Jacob lived with this name his entire life, but he could no longer be defined by this meaning. God not only blessed Jacob with his own covenant blessing, but he also blessed him by finally changing his name.

Biblical names are so important because they not only give a title or explain a person's character, but they also speak to the destiny of a person or people. In Hebrew, Israel means "One who struggles with God or one who strives or wins with God."

Jacob and his twelve sons will eventually become the foundation of God's chosen people: the twelve tribes of Israel. Yup, dem disrespectful children, the Israelites! Their destiny surely is one who truly struggles with God and one who prevails with God.

Chapter Twenty-Three
THE REUNION
Genesis Chapter 33

It's. About. To. Go. Down.

SO, BOOM WHAT HAD HAPPENED WAS...

Jacob saw Esau coming with his four hundred homies. In his last attempt for some kind of protection for his family, he divided them into three groups. The first group was his secondary wives. The second group was Leah and her children. The last group had his favorite wife and child, Rachel and Joseph.

Jacob put them behind him and led the way to Esau. As he approached, he went down on his knees and bowed to the earth seven times, moving forward each time, trying his best to show respect and honor to Esau until he got right up to him.

Before he could reach Esau, Esau *ran* up on him and drop kicked him in the throat!

Nah! That's not what happened. Sorry, I got a little too excited for revenge. Esau *ran* up on him and *hugged* him! Esau embraced him and kissed him over and over again. The twins wept uncontrollably together. (Is someone cutting onions?)

Jacob introduced all of his family to his brother. Then Esau asked, "What are all those flocks as gifts about?" Jacob explained that God had graciously blessed him, and he had more than he could ever need. Esau insisted that he was also blessed and did not need any gifts from Jacob, but eventually, he accepted all the gifts.

Esau wanted to lead Jacob the rest of the way, but Jacob explained that because the flock was young and nursing, they could die if they were pushed too hard. So, Jacob took his time making his way. He built a shelter for the animals and a house for himself until they were able to move on. When he finally arrived in the city of Shechem, he bought some land and pitched his tents there. Jacob finally was at peace. He built an altar and named it El-Elohe-Israel, which means "The God of Israel."

SIP ON THIS TEA: Here's some biblical context to sip on.

El- Elohe- Israel

Let's take a moment to reflect back on an important part of Jacob's story. He just ran away from home, and he is all alone in the wilderness. He has a dream called "Jacob's Ladder." You can flip back to that part of the story if you need to refresh your teacup.

When Jacob wakes from this vision, he builds an altar and makes a vow. He says that if God takes care of him and he's able to return to his family peacefully, *then* he will declare that The Lord is *his* God.

The significance of Jacob erecting an altar and naming it El-Elohe-Israel is so profound. El- Elohe-Israel means "The God of Israel."

Let's break it down.

First, Jacob is now calling himself by his new God-given name, Israel. He peacefully reconciled with his brother Esau. He can finally let go of the shame of living in the shadow of being a supplanter.

Secondly, and most importantly, he is keeping his vow and declaring that the Lord, God Almighty, is *his* God. God was always described as the God of Abraham and Isaac. Jacob, like many of us, based his faith on their relationships with God and didn't have a true personal relationship with the Lord for himself. By naming the altar "God of Israel," he is acknowledging that God kept all His promises to him, and in return, Israel kept his promise and declared the Lord as his one and only God.

Chapter Twenty-Four
THE TREACHERY CONTINUES
GENESIS CHAPTER 34

My Dearest Bible Tea Sippers, after reading the title of this mini cup of Bible Tea surely you are thinking Jacob is up to his treacherous trickery again. I can assure you he is not! However, that doesn't stop his sons from following in their pop's footsteps.

SO, BOOM WHAT HAD HAPPENED WAS...

Jacob and Leah had one daughter named Dinah. One day, Dinah went outside for a girl's night all by herself. Shechem, the sheik of the land of the Shechemites, saw her and decided to take it upon himself to kidnap here and rape her! Afterwards, he tried to win her over, talking bout how much he loved her and stuff. (That poor girl was getting gaslit like a stove.) He really felt like he loved her, so he went to his father and said, "Yo pops! Get me this girl! I'm gonna marry her!"

Now, Jacob heard about what happened to his baby girl. But his sons were out in the field with all his flock, so he was waiting for them to get back before he said or did anything. But before he could do anything, the rapist and his father showed up to Jacob's house!

Now, as soon as her brothers heard what happened, they left that field so fast and were on their way! They were deeply heartbroken and full of rage that Shechem violated their sister and dishonored their father by doing so. When they arrived at the house, Shechem's father, Hamor, greeted them with a proposal.

He explained that his son's soul longed for Dinah. He was so in love that he wanted to marry her. In fact, not only should they give him Dinah, they should make an agreement to combine all their families in arranged marriages. That way, they could all be rich, own all the land, do business together, and create generational wealth.

Shechem decided to actually speak for himself and said, "Let me get on y'all's good side. How 'bout this: I'll give y'all whatever you ask. I'm the Sheik of the land. I got so much money, you can name any bride price, and I'll pay it. All I'm asking for is for y'all to give up your daughter and sister and let her be mine!"

Her brothers were like, "Nah! Y'all Shechemites ain't circumcised. We don't get down like that in our culture. That's disrespectful. Inter-marrying with y'all will bring disgrace on our entire family. However, we would consider your proposal under one condition: If y'all become like us and every single last man in your entire tribe gets snipity snipped, then we will let our daughters marry y'all's sons, and our sons marry y'all's daughters. However, if every man does not consent to getting circumcised, then we will just take Dinah and be out."

Shechem was all hype about their agreement. He wasted no time. He went straight to his home and convinced all the men that Jacob and his sons were such kindhearted, peaceful people. After telling them about the condition of their deal, every single man agreed to get their rims trimmed. (That's some serious convincing.) Shechem didn't know, the brothers was straight lying tho. (Sips tea quietly.)

Now, let's fast forward to the third day after all these foolish, I mean brave men got circumcised.

All of the men were in excruciating pain. They were probably all laid up, trying their best not to move—just a bunch of sitting sore ducks. Well, two of Jacob's sons, Simeon and Levi, snuck into the town like John Wick and Denzel the Equalizer with their swords and schmurdered *every* single man! These brothers done tricked these men into ripping their tips just to turn around and slice and dice them to death!! (This tea is hot!)

They ran up in Shechem's house, killed the rapist and his pops, then rescued their sister Dinah straight outta there. As they were leaving, the other brothers came and looted every man's house, took all of their flock, and kidnapped their wives and children! Jacob's sons robbed thee entire town!

Jacob was highly upset! He couldn't believe that his sons committed such treacherous trickery. He scolded them and warned them that now all the surrounding cities would band together and come after them!

Simeon and Levi weren't trying to hear that tho! They responded, "What?! Were we supposed to just sit back and let him treat our sister like a hoe?" (How are they right and so wrong at the same time. Geez!)

God told Jacob to leave and go to Bethel. So, once again, Jacob found himself running away from the aftermath of some trickery. Jacob told all his sons to get rid of all the false gods and idols they may have stolen. After everyone did a ceremony to purify themselves, he buried all of the idols in the land of the Shechemites.

God caused terror to fall on the people in the surrounding cities, so everyone was too afraid to chase after Jacob and his family. They eventually journeyed south from Bethel, but before they arrived at their next destination, Rachel began to give birth! Yup! Rachel was blessed again with another baby. But poor Rachel was having deadly complications.

Our beautiful Rachel was slowly dying as she gave birth! While she was slowly slipping away, she named her son Ben-oni, which means "son of my sorrow," but Jacob didn't want a sad name, so he changed his twelfth son's name to Benjamin, which means "son of the south." Then Jacob's beautiful Rachel took her last breath.

SIP ON THIS TEA: Here's some biblical context to sip on.

Dinah's Name Meaning

As we learned earlier, Dinah's name means "Judgment" in Hebrew. The Hebrew definition of the term judgment means "to punish, vindicate, and obtain justice for a person." Whoa! Talk about foreshadowing! Dinah's brothers, Simeon and Levi, surely brought judgment on Shechem and his entire town for violating their sister!

However, Jacob was not pleased. They used trickery and ruthlessness to seek revenge. They corrupted the ceremony of circumcision, which represents a sacred covenant with God, to deceive the Shechemites.

Although their motive may seem justified, their story teaches us the dangers of going too far to right a wrong. When it was time for Jacob to give out his blessings to his children, he skipped right over Simeon and Levi for what they did to the Shechemites. They missed out on God's blessing for taking judgment into their own hands.

Chapter Twenty-Five
THE STORY OF JOSEPH
GENESIS CHAPTER 37

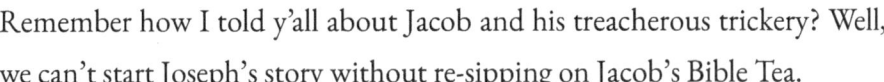

Remember how I told y'all about Jacob and his treacherous trickery? Well, we can't start Joseph's story without re-sipping on Jacob's Bible Tea.

SO, BOOM WHAT HAD HAPPENED WAS...

Jacob was married to the sisters Rachel and Leah. He was in love with Rachel and worked seven long years to win her hand in marriage. But on their wedding night, he learned he got tricked into marrying her not-so-pretty sister Leah. So, he had to work an additional seven long years to finally marry Rachel. Things got really messy! Leah kept popping out babies while Rachel was struggling. Finally, God blessed Rachel with a son. His name was Joseph. Jacob had twelve sons, but Joseph was his favorite.

One day when JoJo was 17 years old, Jacob made him a fancy robe of many colors. Well, this made his brothers super jealous! They couldn't stand Joseph and was always talking to him sideways! To make things worse, JoJo kept having dreams that one day he would rule over his brothers.

One day, he told them this:

Joseph's Dream

"Y'all gotta hear this dream I had!"
Crazy thing, man—wild and mad.
We out in the field, working the land,
Binding up grain with our own hands.
Then boom!—outta nowhere,
I swear it's true,
My sheaf stood tall, like it just knew.
And then y'all's sheaves?
Gathered 'round,
Next thing I know—they bowed down.
What it all means? I can't yet see,
But that dream felt real as can be.

His brothers was like, "So you tryna say you actually gonna rule over us or something?" This made them hate him even more. JoJo didn't care. He just kept telling them about his dreams.

On another day he told them this:

Joseph's Second Dream

"Peep this, y'all! I had another dream!"
Wilder than before—know what I mean?
Eleven stars up in the sky,
Then the sun and moon—man, I can't lie.
They all looked up, then bent down low,
Bowed to me like they already know.

Outta mad respect, outta something deep,
What it all means? Man, it won't let me sleep.

JoJo even told his father about the dream. Jacob was like, "so you tryna say, me, your brothers, and ya mama are actually gonna bow down to the ground, to you?" Jacob rebuked him but he started to wonder if Joseph's dreams had a deeper meaning. (Sips tea silently.) The brothers on the other hand had about enough! They were sick of him always talking bout his lil dreams & struttin around in that colorful lil coat pops gave him.

One day, his brothers were in the field. Jacob sent JoJo to go check on them and then basically come back to snitch on what they were doing. But Joseph got lost in the field and couldn't find them. A stranger asked him what he was looking for. When he told him he was looking for his brothers, the stranger sent him to Dothan to find them.

As JoJo was making his way there, his brothers saw him coming from a distance. They started scheming with each other. They said, "Here comes that dreamer. Let's kill him and throw him into a pit! Then we'll tell Pops that a wild animal killed him. Let's see if he can have his little dreams then." (Bunch of haters) But his oldest brother, Reuben, was like, "Nah, let's not kill him. Just throw him in a pit!" (He was planning to come rescue him later.)

So, when JoJo got to them, they stripped off his Crayola-looking robe and threw him in a pit and left him there. While they were sitting down to have a meal, they saw a caravan of Ishmaelite traders headed to Egypt. So, his trifling brother Judah said, "Ayyoo! Let's not kill him, let's just sell him into slavery!" (Like what!?)

They pulled JoJo out of the pit and sold him for twenty silver shekels. Now, big bro Reuben wasn't there when this happened. So, when he returned, he went straight to the pit to save JoJo but discovered he wasn't there. He was so distraught, he tore his robe in sorrow! He rejoined his brothers and was like, "The young boy isn't in the pit! Where am I gonna hide? 'Cause Pops is going to be pissed!" So, these disrespekful children killed a poor goat, took Joseph's rainbow- looking robe, dipped it in the goat's blood, then took it to their Pops talking about, "We found this…um, could you look at it and see if it's JoJo's?" (Why are they playing these games? Who else got a skittles looking robe?)

Poor Jacob was tore up from the floor up! He said, "It is Joseph's! A wild animal probably tore my baby up to pieces!" Jacob was so distraught, he tore his robe in grief. He put on sackcloth and mourned his son for days. None of his kids could console him, not even his daughter Dinah.

Meanwhile, JoJo really wasn't dead; he is very much alive! However, he is now a slave in Egypt and just got sold to Potiphar, the captain of Pharaoh's royal guard. (Sips tea a little louder.)

SIP ON THIS TEA: Here's some biblical context to sip on.

Joseph's Robe of Many Colors

Biblical scholars say his brothers weren't jealous just because the robe had many colors. In fact, it was a long sleeve tunic. Historically, a long sleeve tunic indicated royalty and privilege. This signified Joseph was not expected to do hard labor in the field like his brothers. Jacob's favoritism was evident every time his sons had to go and do all the hard work while JoJo was spying on them, snitching on them, and never having to lift a finger wearing his fancy little robe.

Ishmaelite Caravan

The Ishmaelites are the descendants of Ishmael. You know, Abraham's first son that he had with his maid Hagar because his wife Sarah was impatient and didn't wait on God to bless her with her own child. (Go back and sip on that tea in Genesis chapter 16 if you need to refresh your teacup.) Yup, we're talking about that Ishmael. Joseph got sold to his descendants! Oh, the irony! Why did he get sold to them? Essentially because of this family's generational pattern of favoritism. The Ishmaelites would have never existed if Abraham would not have kicked out poor Hagar and her son. Abraham is Joseph's great-grandaddy. Isaac clearly was Abraham's favorite son. Jacob was Isaac's favorite son, and JoJo was Jacob's favorite son. All this favoritism led to so much pain and suffering for this family.

Twenty Coins of Silver

Joseph was sold for 20 shekels of silver. The conversion rate in modern times would be $2.20 per Shekel. That means his brothers sold poor JoJo for $44 dollars. If only they knew they were selling him from the pit to the palace!

Chapter Twenty-Six
TAMAR & JUDAH
GENESIS CHAPTER 38: DAUGHTER IN-LAWS REVENGE

You might be thinking, how did we get here? Why is there this random story smack dab in the middle of Joseph's story? Don't worry, My Dearest Bible Tea Sippers. Trust me, it all connects! Nothing is random with God.

SO, BOOM WHAT HAD HAPPENED WAS...

Judah, yes Judah, Joseph's trifling brother that said, "Let's not kill him, let's just *sell him into slavery*," had three sons. Their names were Er, Onan, and Shelah. Well, Er got married to this chick named Tamar, but Er was straight evil and God was like, "Nah, Bruh." So, boom, he died! Judah was like, "Onan, my second, go to Tamar and perform your duties under the levirate law as a brother-in-law." Onan wasn't feeling this at all!

You see, traditionally, this meant that if he ever had kids, they would be considered his brother Er's heirs and not his own. So, whenever him and Tamar would be knocking boots, he was like, "My pull-out game is strong" and "spilled his seed" on the ground. God was like, "Oh, you are being disobedient," nah Bruh. So, boom, *he* died!

Now, Judah is looking at Tamar like, "Why, every time my sons are with *you*, they die?" So, he told her, "Go back to your father as a widow and wait for my third son, Shelah, to grow up. Then I will send for you, and you will get married. (He was lying tho.) So, Tamar sadly went back home to her father's house.

Yeeeaaarrrss passed, and Judah's wife died. When his time of mourning was over, he traveled to go shear his sheep at Timnah. Tamar's friends were like, "Girl, your father-in-law is in town." So, Tamar finally took off her widow clothes, put on a veil, and sat at the gate on the road leading to Timnah. But when she saw Judah, she also saw that Shelah been had his glow-up! She was never given to him like Judah promised!

When Judah saw her, he thought she was a prostitute because of her veil. So, he was like, "Hey, shawty, come be with me." Tamar was like, "Um, whatchu gonna give me to get with me?" He was like, "I'll send you a goat." (Chille, don't even ask.) Tamar was like, "I need a security deposit, 'cause people be lying. So let me get your seal, chord, and staff until I get my goat." So, Judah gave them to her, and they did the do. When they were done, Tamar got up and left. She quickly removed her veil, put her widow clothes back on, and went back to her father's house.

Afterwards, Judah sent his friend with the goat to go get his security deposit back. His friend went all around town with that goat asking everybody, "Where was that hoe that be sitting by the gate?" But everybody kept saying, "Ain't no prostitutes around here! (Chiile, this tea is getting hot!)

His friend told Judah that he couldn't find her, and everyone was saying there were no prostitutes in this town! Judah was like, "She can keep those things because I'm about to be the laughingstock around here if anyone finds out." About three months later, Judah heard that Tamar was out in the streets acting like a prostitute and now she's pregnant. (Oop!) Judah got mad and was like, "Bring her out, we're about to burn her to death as punishment!

She is supposed to be a widow and wait for my son, not be out in these streets hoeing!"

As they were bringing her out of the house to put her to death, she grabbed the three things she kept as her security deposit. Tamar was like, "Please don't kill me, listen, the father of my baby is the owner of this seal, chord, and staff, tell Judah to look at them carefully!" (Sips tea cracking up.)

Immediately Judah knew that these were his things, which meant that Tamar was that veiled women he slept with and that he was the baby daddy. Judah had a change of heart real quick. He realized that Tamar was more righteous than he was because he promised to give her to his son Shelah, and he never kept his word. Judah and Tamar never hooked up again.

When it was time to give birth, Tamar had twins. While she was pushing, the first one stuck out his hand, so the midwife tied a scarlet ribbon around his wrist. But he pulled his hand back in, and his brother was born first. They named the first-born twin Perez, which means "breached." When the other twin with the scarlet ribbon was born, they named him Zerah, which means "brightness."

SIP ON THIS TEA: Here's some biblical context to sip on.

Tamar Sent to Her Father's House

Biblical scholars say that, according to Middle Assyrian laws, if a man has no son over ten years old, he can perform the levirate marriage himself. That means he can marry the woman; however, if he chooses not to, the woman is declared a widow, and she is free to marry again.

This is imperative because, during these times, women could not provide for themselves and relied heavily on their husbands for survival. But Judah didn't marry Tamar! Instead, he sent her home to her father's house as a "widow in waiting." She was waiting for Shelah to become of age. She could not remarry, and she had to stay chaste until death or until he came to get her.

We know that Judah had no intention of giving his last baby boy to Tamar. He literally doomed her to a lonely life where she could not provide for herself. That is why his change of heart is so significant. Not only did he not kill her, but he admitted she was more righteous than him, and he gave her back her freedom by allowing her to secure a place in his family.

The Significance of the Birth of Perez

Although the twin's conception was surrounded by scandal, their birth is significant. Later on, in the book of Ruth, we discover that Ruth is from the lineage of Perez. We also know that Ruth is in the lineage of King David. And most importantly, we know that our Lord and Savior, Jesus Christ, comes from the lineage of King David.

No wonder this story appears in the middle of Joseph's story. It's an essential part of the redemption story. It proves once again how God takes our mess and turns it into a message for His Glory. God loves taking a nobody and making them a somebody in front of everybody!

Chapter Twenty-Seven
THE PRISON
GENESIS CHAPTER 39

Remember in Part 1 how I told y'all Joseph's brothers were jealous of him? They were sick of him always talking about his little dreams of ruling over them one day. They were jealous he was pop's favorite and always strutting around in that coat that looked like a bag of Skittles. So, what did they do? They *sold him into slavery,* then lied to their pops by telling him his favorite son was dead! *(Um, um, um!)* But we know he wasn't dead. He was taken to Egypt and sold as a slave. Let's keep sipping.

SO, BOOM WHAT HAD HAPPENED WAS...

Joseph got sold to Potiphar, the captain of the Pharaoh's Royal Guard. But God was with him! Even though he was a slave, he became highly successful. *Everything* our boy touched prospered. I'm talking about Potiphar became *rich* rich! He realized it was because of JoJo and the God that was with him. So, Potiphar made Joseph his personal servant. From the time he made JoJo the overseer, the Lord continued to bless *everythang* that Joseph touched.

Now, Joseph was very handsome. He was attractive not just by how he looked, but by how he carried himself, too. Do you know who else noticed JoJo was good with everything he touched? Potiphar's thirsty behind trifling little wife. She started setting up thirst traps for JoJo, begging him to come lay with her. But *every* time JoJo was like, "Nah, you dusty hoe! (Ok he didn't really say that, but he probably wanted to.) He said, "Me and my God don't get down like that. Plus, I could never do that to my mans Potiphar! I could never do such an evil thing and sin against God." But she didn't listen! She pursued JoJo persistently, day after day. (Just parched and thirsty!) And every time Joseph told her no!

One day JoJo came in the house, and no one was there not even the servants (Red flag Bruh, run!) Here comes dusty thirsty home girl talkin bout, "Come lay with me Joey" and grabbed him by his robe. (Outer coat thingy) Chiile! JoJo ran up out of there so fast he left his robe right in her crusty molester hands. When she realized she still had his robe she had the nerve to yell to everyone outside, "Look that Hebrew that my husband brought up in my house tried to rape me! When I screamed, he left his robe and ran away."

When Potiphar got home, she told her lil lie, and Potiphar was so mad he threw our boy JoJo in Jail! (Shaking my head) But God was with him. In prison, the Lord gave him favor in the sight of the warden. The warden put him in charge of all the other prisoners. Now, sometime later, the Pharoah got really mad at his cup bearer and his baker and threw them into prison. The warden put JoJo in charge of them too.

Well, it just so happened that one night the cup bearer and the baker both had dreams. The next morning Joseph came to them and realized they both looked sad. They said, "We both had dreams, but there is no one to interpret them. (Pushes up glasses and sips tea loudly.) JoJo says, "Don't interpretations belong to God? Tell them to me.

So, the cup bearer told this dream:

The Cup Bearer's Dream
"Listen, man, I had this dream last night,
" Clear as day, like a vision in sight.
Right in front of me—a grapevine stood,
Three branches strong, full of life, full of good.
It budded, it bloomed—BOOM, just like that,
Ripe grapes popped out, nothing holding them back.
Then all of a sudden, in my hand so real,
Pharaoh's cup, gold shining, royal appeal.
So, I took them grapes, squeezed them tight,
Let the juice flow red, rich, and bright.
Poured it up, placed it right in his hand,
What it all means? Man, I don't understand.

Joseph was like, "Ok the three branches represent three days. Within three days the Pharoah is going to restore you to your position as the cup bearer. You're gonna be alright. Listen tho, please do me a favor. Remember me! Mention me to the Pharoah so I can get out of here. I was taken from the land of the Hebrews, and I don't even belong here."

Since the cup bearer's dream interpretation was so good the baker was all hype to tell his dream:

The Baker's Dream
"Man, listen—this dream got me shook."
Had me seeing things, gotta take a look.
Three baskets stacked, sitting on my head,
Full of baked goods, finest bread.
Top one loaded—pastries and more,

Fit for Pharaoh, straight to his door.
But then—birds came down from the sky,
Snatching the food, man, I don't know why.
What it all means? I just can't see,
But something 'bout it ain't sitting right with me.

Joseph was like, "Oh ok sooooo… um… your dream means that in three days the Pharoah is going to hang you from the gallows. They won't even bury you, and the birds are going to eat your dead flesh." (Yikes!)

Sure enough, three days later, it was the Pharoah's birthday. He threw a feast for all his servants and took the two men out of prison. The Pharoah restored the cupbearer back to his position, and the cupbearer put his cup right in Pharoah's hand. But Pharoah hung the baker just like Joseph said he would. The cupbearer totally forgot to mention Joseph to Pharoah like he promised. In fact, our boy JoJo wouldn't cross his mind again for another two whole years.

SIP ON THIS TEA: Here's some biblical context to sip on.

But God Was with Him

This phrase is woven throughout Joseph's story. It seems like, even in his darkest, most frightening moments, when others abandon him, God never does. When his own brothers sell him into slavery, God is with him. When he is in Potiphar's house as a slave, he is still successful because God is with him. When Potiphar believes his lying wife and throws Joseph into prison, God is with him. He finds favor with the warden because God is with him. This is a great reminder that when we find ourselves in pits, prisons, or even in prosperity, God is always with us. He will never leave nor forsake us.

Don't interpretations belong to God?

Biblical scholars point out that when the two men say, "but there is no one to interpret our dreams," it's because historically, in Egypt, dream interpretations were done by trained men, such as magicians and wise men. By Joseph saying, "Don't interpretations belong to God?" he is declaring that this has nothing to do with science or magic. There is no specialized training. God is the only one who interprets dreams and reveals them through His chosen prophets. In many ways, this is a lightbulb moment. Years ago, Joseph told his dreams in an arrogant way, not acknowledging they came from God. Now he realizes this divine gift is from God, and he is being used as a vessel to interpret them.

Chapter Twenty-Eight
THE PALACE
GENESIS CHAPTER 41

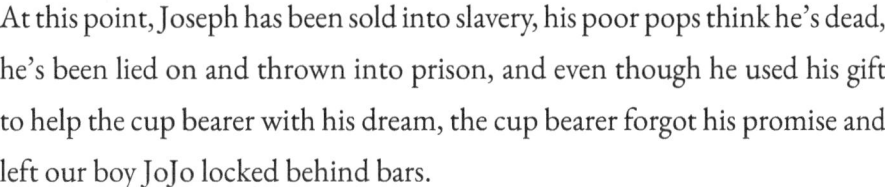

At this point, Joseph has been sold into slavery, his poor pops think he's dead, he's been lied on and thrown into prison, and even though he used his gift to help the cup bearer with his dream, the cup bearer forgot his promise and left our boy JoJo locked behind bars.

SO, BOOM WHAT HAD HAPPENED WAS...

It's a whole two years later and one night the Pharaoh has a dream. (Sips tea while smirking.)

The Pharoah had this dream:

Pharoah's Dream
Pharoah was standing by the Nile—still, calm, deep,
When boom—out the water, seven cows creep.
Not just any cows—fat, sleek, prime,
Grazing in the grass like life was divine.
But then—out the same water, something ain't right,
Seven more come, ugly, sunken, tight.
Skeleton-thin, eyes wild and wide,
Lookin' like death, hunger inside.

Then it happened—no warning, no sound,
Them bony beasts took the fat ones down.
Ate 'em up like starving fiends,
Left nothing behind—not a bone, not a dream.
Pharaoh sat up—sweat on his brow,
But sleep pulled him back, another vision now.
Seven stalks rise—golden, full, strong,
Heavy with grain, nothing seems wrong.
But then—boom! From the dirt came more,
Seven thin ones—withered, poor.
They stretched, they reached, they swallowed 'em whole,
Like time itself had lost control.
Pharaoh woke up, heart beating fast,
Visions so vivid, how long will they last?
A warning, a sign, or just consequence?
What does it mean? Man, make it make sense.

The next morning, the Pharaoh was so disturbed that he called all the magicians and wise men of Egypt to come and interpret his dream. Pharaoh told them his dream, but none of these phony people could tell him what his dream was about. Then the cupbearer was like, "Oh, my bad. You know what? I forgot to tell you this: You remember two years ago when you were mad at me and threw me into prison? Well, me and the baker had a dream the same night, and this young Hebrew dude interpreted our dreams. *Everything* happened exactly like he said. He said the baker was gonna get hanged, and I was gonna be restored as your cupbearer." (Geez finally! It took you long enough to remember our boy. Thank you!)

So, the Pharaoh called for Joseph. They took JoJo out of prison and let him shave himself and change his clothes so he could look presentable. Then

Pharaoh said, "I had a dream," in his MLK voice, "and there is no one who could interpret it. I heard that you understand dreams." But JoJo was like, "Nah, it's not me, it's God who will interpret the dream through me." So, Pharaoh told him both of his dreams.

Then Joseph said, "These aren't two dreams; they are one and have the same interpretation. God is telling you what He is about to do. The seven good cows and the seven good ears of grain mean seven good years. The seven anorexic-looking cows and the dried-up seven ears of grain are seven years of famine and hunger. The fact that you had the dream twice means that God is serious that this is about to happen. I need you to listen to me carefully!

Joseph's Instructions
God said there's bout to be seven years of overflow,
Egypt gonna prosper, the land gonna glow.
But right after that, the famine will hit,
So bad, so dry, they'll forget they were rich.
What you need to do is move real wise,
Get ahead of the drought before hunger rise.
Find a man—sharp, trusted, and strong,
Put him in charge so nothing goes wrong.
Appoint governors, spread them wide,
Every region gotta keep food inside.
One-fifth of the crops? Lock that down,
No touching, no stealing, don't play around.
Cuz when the seven years of famine come through,
That reserve gonna save the whole land, it's true.
No one starving, no one left dry,
God gave the warning—act now or later cry.

Pharaoh was impressed. He said, "Can we even find a man like this in all of Egypt who has the divine spirit of God like this dude Joseph? Since your God showed this to you, you do it!" Pharaoh put JoJo in charge of everything! He told Joseph that the only person higher than him in all of Egypt was the Pharaoh himself. Then Pharaoh took off his ring, put it on JoJo's hand, dressed him up in fancy, official-looking clothes, and iced out his neck with chains.

He then had people ride around with Joseph on a chariot yelling out, "Everybody bow down to Joseph and give him mad respect." (Sounds familiar, don't it? Sips tea while staring at you.)

Joseph was 30 years old when he became the second in command and ruler over all of Egypt. He performed his duty like only JoJo could, and Egypt prospered. Meanwhile, he got married and had two sons. The first one he named Manasseh, which means, "cause to forget." He praised God for helping him forget about all his heartache from his brothers' betrayal. The second son he named Ephraim, which means, "fruitfulness," because God caused him to be fruitful and successful in a foreign land.

Finally, after those seven good years, the seven years of famine began, just like JoJo said it would. The famine was so severe, it didn't just happen in Egypt; it spread to surrounding countries. People were starving from all over. They were coming in flocks to see Joseph in Egypt so they could buy grain from the reserve in the storehouses. You know who else was starving and needed to come to Egypt to buy grain? Joseph's eleven brothers.

SIP ON THIS TEA: Here's some biblical context to sip on.

You Do It

Biblical scholars love diving into Joseph's use of his gifts. They often focus heavily on his prophetic gift of interpretation. However, when we sip on the list of spiritual gifts, it is important to note that Joseph's spiritual gift of administration is essential to not only his success but saving others. Using our spiritual gifts expresses our faith in God and helps build someone's else's faith in God as well.

If you don't know your spiritual gifts you can also take an online assessment.

Chapter Twenty-Nine
THE PURPOSE
GENESIS CHAPTER 42

Joseph is now the ruler of Egypt, second to command to the Pharaoh himself. We know the poor baby got sold into slavery at the age of 17. We don't know how long he spent in Potiphar's house before he got kicked out for not giving the D to Potiphar's trifling wife. But what we do know, My Dearest Bible Tea Sippers, is that he spent two years in prison, and he was 30 years old when he became the ruler. So, if the math is mathing, I think it's safe to say he hasn't seen his family in 13 years. That all about to change!

SO, BOOM WHAT HAD HAPPENED WAS...

Jacob heard that there was corn and grain in Egypt. So, he said to his sons, "Why y'all just sitting around here staring at each other instead of actually doing something? There is grain in Egypt! I need y'all to go there and buy some, so we don't starve and die!" So, Jacob sent ten of his sons, but he didn't send his youngest son Benjamin because that was the only child he had left with his favorite wife Rachel. He already lost his favorite son Joseph the last time he sent him somewhere. Ain't no way he was bout to send his other favorite baby boy anywhere to get hurt or killed by a wild animal too.

Now when the brothers got to Egypt, they had to go see the ruler in order to buy grain. So, they came before him and bowed down with their faces to the ground. (Sips tea loudly and almost chokes.) When the ruler JoJo, saw his brothers, he recognized them immediately, but they had no clue who he was. He remembered his dreams he had as a young boy and started treating them like he didn't know them. He started coming at their necks like, "Y'all look like a bunch a spies! Y'all just coming to our land so you can see how bad were doing!" They was all like, "Nah were just brothers, we come from the same dad straight outta Canaan. There are really twelve of us but our youngest brother is with our pops and our other brother died."

JoJo was like, "Nope! Y'all are spies and I'm bout to see if y'all lying! Nobody is leaving until somebody brings that younger brother y'all keep talking bout here! So, choose one to go back to get him but the rest are staying here! Then JoJo threw them in prison for three days. (Savage!) On the third day JoJo said, "Alright I'm a God-fearing man and y'all might be telling the truth. So, here's what we bout to do. One of y'all is gonna stay in prison. Everyone else can buy grain to take back home. However, I'm not letting the one in prison go until y'all come back here with that youngest brother to prove y'all aren't lying spies or I'm gonna kill all of y'all."

The brothers start freaking out and talking to each other in Hebrew, but they don't know that JoJo can understand them. And JoJo is just playing along using an interrupter acting like he don't know what's really being said. (I'm cracking up over here.) They are like, "Yooo, this is what we get. This is happening because of what we did to Joseph all dem years ago!" Reuben was like, "Man I told y'all not to hurt him! Nobody ever listens to me. His blood is on our hands and now were gonna have to pay for it in blood." Joseph got up and left the room and started crying. (Ohh JoJo!) When he came back, he took their brother Simeon and tied him up. Then JoJo gave his servants a secret command to fill up all of their sacks with corn and put their money back in the sacks too.

The brothers left to go back home but when they got to an inn one of them opened up his sack to pay and he noticed that all of his money was back. Chiile, they were shooketh!

When they got back to Canaan, they told Pops what happened. They were like, "The ruler of Egypt thinks that we are spies. He was talking all rough to us, and he is holding Simeon hostage until we bring Benji back to him to prove we ain't lying, or he finna kill us!" When the brothers opened all of their sacks, they each saw that all of the money they thought they spent to buy the corn was now back in their sacks! They were scared out of their minds. Jacob was like, "So my Joseph is gone, now Simeon is gone, and now you're telling me I gotta give up Benji too!"

Reuben said, "Pops, just give Benji to me, and I will take him there, and I promise I will bring him back. I put that on my son's lives!" But Jacob was like, "Ain't no way I'm sending my only child left that I had with my beautiful Rachel anywhere with you. If something happens to him, I'm finna die!"

Now, sometime later, the famine is getting crazy in Canaan. Jacob's family had eaten up all the grain and corn they bought from Egypt. It took the brothers forever to convince Pops to let them take Benji with them so they could buy a little more food. When the brothers got to Egypt and JoJo saw his baby brother Benji was with them, he had his servants prepare a meal for them and invited them to his house. Now the brothers were scared because, why else would they be taken to the ruler's house? They thought it was about the money that was in their sacks the last time they came.

So, they told the steward of the house, "Look, the last time we were here, when we opened our sacks, we discovered that all of our money was in it. We promise we have no clue how it got back in there. So, this time we brought extra money with us and that money back as well."

The steward was like, "Don't sweat it. The God of your father restored that money back to you." He brought out Simeon and took them all inside. When JoJo finally got home, all his brothers once again bowed before him. He asked them, "Is your old father that you talked about still alive, and is this the younger brother you were telling me about?"

The brothers told him that Pops was still surviving the famine and yes, this was their lil bro Benji.

Now, as soon as JoJo looked at Benji, his baby brother—the only brother out of all his brothers that was also his mama's child—he got all mushy and had to leave the room again to go cry.

Once he washed his face and got himself together, he said, "Let's eat." So, the servants served Joseph first, but then the steward sat all the brothers down according to their birth order.

The brothers were looking at each other like, "Ayo, what is happening? How is it possible that they know our birth order?" Then Joseph had the servants give them all big portions from his table, but he gave Benji five times as much food as everybody else.

JoJo knew the brothers would soon have to leave. Once again, he was on some secretive type time. He told his servants to fill each of their sacks full of grain, put all of their money back, but this time also take his personal silver cup and put it in Benji's sack. So, the next morning when the brothers were heading out on their donkeys, as soon as they got a little far away, JoJo sent his steward running after them! He was like, "Y'all are grimy! Is this how y'all pay back kindness with being shady? One of y'all took my master's drinking cup. This is a major crime!"

The brothers were like, "Nah, we ain't no thieves! We just told you that money was returned to us the last time we were here and we had no clue how it happened. What we look like now, stealing silver from your Master's house? In fact, we're so confident that none of us took it, that if you find the cup, let that man be put to death."

The steward was like, "Bet. Whoever has the cup, I'm gonna do exactly what you said, and the rest will go free." (Y'all did not think this through.) So, they emptied all of their sacks, and the steward starts searching through them, going from the oldest to the youngest.

And lo and behold, when he gets to the last bag, sure nuff, that silver cup was right in Benji's sack!

The brothers started wildin' out and tore their clothes in grief! They all got back on their donkeys and headed back to the city to Joseph's house. As soon as JoJo saw them, he started tripping! He was yelling like, "Oh, y'all done did it now! Don't y'all know I got divine knowledge of stuff? Did you not think I would find out?" So, his brother Judah was like, "Look, what can we even say? How can we even clear our names? Just take us all as your slaves."

But JoJo was like, "Nah, I'm not gonna do that. But whoever stole my cup, he's gonna be my slave. The rest can go back home to y'all geezer father!"

So, Judah starts freaking out, and he's like, "Look, my Lord, I know you're not the Pharaoh, but you're equal to him, so I'm gonna talk to you with respect, like I'm talking to him. Do you have any brothers or a father? Because if you do, you gotta understand that we can't leave our baby brother Benjamin here. Remember how we told you our father is very old? Well, our lil brother is his favorite because he had him in his old age. He is really special because he is the only child left from his mother because his other brother died. Now, we tried to tell you before that we couldn't bring him here because if something happened to him, our father would die! But you made us bring him anyway. We can't go back home without Benji. Our pops already lost one son, this is going to kill him! Please just take me instead!"

At this point, Joseph couldn't take it anymore. He could not control himself in front of everyone. He told all his servants to get out! Chiilee, JoJo started weeping so loud that all the servants in the house could hear him anyway! He turned to his brothers and said, "It's me. I am Joseph. Is Pops really still alive?" His brothers were stuck! They couldn't believe it was really him. They just stood there speechless. So, JoJo started talking to them in Hebrew.

He said:

Joseph's Big Reveal
Come closer! Look at me. It's really me!
I am Joseph—your brother—the one y'all sold into slavery.
But don't be angry, don't hold that weight,
What you meant for harm, God used to elevate.
It wasn't you that sent me here,
It was God! Let that be clear.
He placed me ahead, He set the stage.
So when famine came, we'd be saved from the grave.
Five more years—the hunger ain't done,
But through His plan, I'm the chosen one.
Ruler of Egypt, set in place,
So our family survives by His mercy and grace.

Then he grabbed Benji and started crying and hugging him. Benji started crying, then errbody started hugging and crying! (And now I'm crying!) When the Pharaoh heard what happened, he was so happy for Joseph. He told his brothers to load up their animals, go back home, and bring everybody back with them. He was about to give them the best land in all of Egypt.

So, JoJo loaded up all these wagons with provisions for their trip home. He gave them each a change of clothing, but he gave Benji five new outfits and 300 pieces of silver. ('cause he's his favorite.) When the brothers got back home, they told their Pops that Joseph is still alive, and he is the ruler over all of Egypt. Chille, Jacob almost had a heart attack.

When they explained everything and he saw all them wagons with them, he said, "Alright, I believe y'all. I'm gonna go see my baby boy before I die." And he did. And that, My Dearest Bible Tea Sippers, is the end of Genesis.

SIP ON THIS TEA: Here are some personal reflections to sip on.

What's Your Tea: Thoughts, Emotions. and Actions

In life, we often find ourselves in dark pits. Now, if I'm being honest, sometimes we're the ones who got ourselves thrown into those pits. But no matter what pit you find yourself in, it's important to remember that God is always with you. Oftentimes, we spend too much time wallowing in self-pity that we can't see past our hurt. It's hard to see the purpose if we're focused solely on our pain.

My Dearest Bible Tea Sippers, may I offer you a perspective change? Maybe your pit was protection. Maybe what felt like slavery was teaching you how to serve others over yourself. Maybe the lies told about you were so your character could speak louder than your accusations. Maybe your family's betrayal was what you needed to become the generational curse breaker.

When you change your perspective by focusing on learning what God's purpose is for your pain, maybe, just maybe, you can get yourself up out of that pit.

What life lessons did you learn from Joseph's story? Take time to journal your T.E.A. Get all your *thoughts* together, explore your *emotions*, and apply Godly *actions*.

AFTERWORD

My Dearest Bible Tea Sippers,

Whew! We've sipped, we've reflected, and we've seen just how real, raw, and relevant the Book of Genesis is. But before you put this book down and move on, let's sit with it for a moment. Let's really soak in the tea. Genesis isn't just a collection of ancient stories about people who lived thousands of years ago. It's a mirror. A reflection of us—our struggles, our choices, our brokenness, and most importantly, our desperate need for God.

Every single person we met in Genesis had their flaws on full display. Adam and Eve fumbled paradise. Cain let jealousy turn him into a murderer. Noah saved his family but later embarrassed himself. Abraham had faith but Sarah lost hope. Lot's wife refused to leave behind what was toxic. Rebekah and Jacob scammed their own blood. Judah tried to play Tamar, but ended up playing himself. And our boy JoJo? Yeah, he was betrayed, abandoned, and lied on—but let's not act like he was flawless. Bragging about dreams, flaunting that favor...God had to humble him before He could elevate him. The pit wasn't just punishment—it was preparation.

The truth is, we are no different from them. Maybe you've made decisions that have distanced you from God. Maybe you've lied, manipulated, envied, doubted, ran, or looked back when He told you to move forward. Maybe you've been through pain so deep you felt forgotten. But if Genesis teaches us anything, it's that God's hand is always moving. Even in the mess. Even in the dysfunction. Even when we don't see it, He is writing redemption into the story.

Genesis started with Adam and Eve losing paradise and dooming the human race, but it ended with Joseph in a position of power, restoring the very family that betrayed him. That is grace. That is mercy. That is the promise that God is not done with you yet. So, I leave you with this question: What tea is your life spilling right now? Is it a story of running from God? A story of struggle? A story of transformation? No matter where you are in the journey, remember this—Genesis is only the beginning of the story.

And so is this moment for you.

The same God who walked with Adam, spared Noah, called Abraham, wrestled with Jacob, and elevated Joseph is still writing your story. So, sip the tea, learn the lessons, and let God lead you into your next chapter. Oh, speaking of the next chapter, stay tuned for *Bible Tea Volume 2: The Exodus*. But that's another tea for another day. Ain't no tea like Bible Tea, hunty.

~ Kaydene Grant
Coach Kbeau2ful

THE CAST LIST

Because the tea was hot from the beginning.

Adam–First Man

- Had one job. Failed.

- Loves gardening but lets his woman do all the work.

- Blame game champion—it's always someone else's fault.

Eve – First Woman

- Enjoys deep convos with snakes.

- Tried one piece of fruit and changed human history.

- Had one job. Also failed.

The Serpent – Professional Liar

- Smooth talker but ruins lives.

- Favorite phrase: "Did God really say?"

- 10/10 manipulation skills.

Cain & Abel – Sibling Rivalry Gone Wrong

- Cain: Easily offended, terrible conflict resolution skills.
- Abel: Minding his business until he wasn't.

Noah – The Boat Builder

- Saved humanity and a bunch of animals.
- Knows his way around a hammer and some wine.
- Likes long cruises and fresh starts.

Ham, Shem, Japheth – Noah's Sons

- Ham: Walked in on Noah's worst moment and told everybody. Snitching at its worst.
- Shem & Japheth: Covered for their dad… literally.

Nimrod – "King" of the First Clout Chase

- Built the Tower of Babel just to go viral.
- Didn't know God had Google Translate on lock.

Abraham – The Father of Many Nations

- Pulled the "She's my sister" trick twice.
- Had a baby at 100—because God's timing ain't ours.
- Faith was strong, but his patience. Questionable.

Sarah – Wife of Abraham, Laughs at God's Promises

- Told her husband to sleep with the maid.
- Mad when it actually worked.
- Got the last laugh when she had a baby at 90 years old.

Hagar – The Original Baby Mama

- Didn't sign up for the drama but got all of it.
- Ran away but got sent back.
- Son became the father of a whole other nation.

Lot – Needs a New GPS System

- Moved to Sodom and ignored all the red flags.
- Almost gave his daughters to a mob—sir?!
- Had to be dragged out of destruction.

Lot's Wife – Salty & Stuck in the Past

- God: "Don't look back." Her: Looks back. Now she's salty.

Lot's Daughters – Terrible Problem Solvers

- Thought the world was ending… so they got their dad drunk.
- The reason we have the Moabites and Ammonites. (Yikes!)

Isaac – Daddy's Boy Turned Rich Farmer

- Almost got sacrificed like a rotisserie chicken.

- Favorite move? Copying his dad's bad habits.

Rebekah – Team Jacob

- Mastermind of family betrayal.

- Favorite son? Jacob, duh.

- Probably ghosted Esau after the birthright scam.

Esau & Jacob – The Messy Twins

- Esau: Traded his whole inheritance for soup. (Sir?)

Jacob – Full of treacherous trickery and wrestled an angel.

- Became Israel—God really be working on folks.

Laban – Ultimate Hustler

- Scammed his own nephew into 14 years of free labor.

- Believes in "family discounts" (But only when he's winning).

Leah & Rachel – The First Sister wives: Love Triangle

- Leah: The first wife, but not the favorite.

- Rachel: The favorite wife but struggled to have kids.

- Both got played by their own father.

Judah & Tamar – Messy Family Ties

- Judah: Tried to play Tamar, got played instead.

- Tamar: Finessed her way into the family tree of Jesus.

Joseph – The Dreamer with a Glow-Up

- Favorite child? Obviously.

- Had visions of power, got sold as a slave by his own brothers.

- Went from prison to palace—a true "God did it" story.

www.ingramcontent.com/pod-product-compliance
Lightning Source LLC
Chambersburg PA
CBHW051327110526
44582CB00003B/75